VACCINATION FOR SURVIVAL IN CORPORATE WORLD

DR KAMALJEET KAUR

Clever Fox®
PUBLISHING
Chennai • Bangalore

CLEVER FOX PUBLISHING
Chennai, India

Published by CLEVER FOX PUBLISHING 2025

ISBN: 978-93-7500-842-2

CONTENTS

FOREWORD

Starting and scaling a business is exhilarating, but it exposes you to constant uncertainty, pressure, and tough decisions. Often, the biggest challenges aren't external—they are internal.

Dr. Kamaljeet Kaur Siddhu's "Vaccination for Survival in the Corporate World" provides a blueprint to strengthen your mental, emotional, and strategic immunity. Her "career vaccines" are precisely the tools every entrepreneur, founder, and professional needs to navigate high-pressure environments without losing sight of wellbeing and purpose.

Dr. Siddhu's work is more than a guide; it's a form of protection and renewal for the corporate soul. I'm confident it will inspire readers to lead with resilience, empathy, and balance in an ever-changing world.

– Sarbjit Singh Gill,

Vice President Sikh Society of Manitoba, Canada &

Women in corporate spaces often face unique challenges—from breaking glass ceilings to balancing career ambitions with personal responsibilities.

Dr. Kamaljeet Kaur Siddhu's "Vaccination for Survival in the Corporate World" is an empowering guide that addresses these challenges head-on. Her insights on resilience, self-advocacy, and strategic growth offer every professional the tools to thrive, regardless of gender or background.

This book is both inspiring and practical—a must-have for women leaders and aspirants alike.

Meenakshi Ohlan,
Director IT at Hewlett Packard Enterprise

In a globalized corporate environment, adaptability is as critical as expertise. Leaders today must navigate cultural differences, technological disruptions, and shifting organizational priorities.

Dr. Kamaljeet Kaur Siddhu's "Vaccination for Survival in the Corporate World" offers timeless strategies that are both universal and actionable. Her "career vaccines" help professionals anticipate challenges, build resilience, and position themselves for sustainable growth in any context.

This echoes Kamaljeet's attitude towards continuous improvement at work - be prepared 'as change is the only constant.'

For anyone seeking a competitive edge in today's corporate ecosystem, this book is indispensable.

– Siddharth Nivsarkar,
Managing partner - Ameet Lubricants and Chemicals;
Past - founder/CEO at Doodle Designs private limited

Dr. Kamaljeet Kaur Sidhu's "Vaccination for Survival in Corporate World" is a groundbreaking guide for anyone navigating the demanding and ever-changing landscape of professional life. Drawing upon the ingenious metaphor of vaccination, Dr. Sidhu translates the language of biological immunity into a practical, empowering toolkit for achieving what she calls "career immunity." Each chapter is a strategic dose—a skill, mindset, or habit—carefully crafted to help professionals tackle the stressors, uncertainties, and opportunities that define the modern workplace.

This book stands apart by demystifying corporate success, breaking it down into relatable stories, actionable prescriptions, and clear frameworks. Dr. Sidhu's approach is refreshingly accessible—whether you are a fresh graduate, a rising manager, or a seasoned leader. She challenges readers not merely to survive but to thrive—adapting, collaborating, and leading with resilience and integrity.

Above all, Dr. Sidhu's work is a testament to the power of preparation, continuous learning, and authentic connection. With this book, she offers not just tactics for career advancement, but a lasting immunization against the setbacks and stagnation of corporate life. Dive in, and let your journey toward full career immunity begin.

– Ankur Jain,
Co-Founder Sunstone Eduversity

"I just finished reading Vaccination for Survival in the Corporate World by Dr. Kamaljeet Kaur Siddhu, and it's a game-changer. The old rules are out; success is now about adaptability and resilience. This book doesn't just tell you that—it gives you the blueprint for how to do it. Siddhu breaks down complex ideas into actionable 'doses' that are easy to digest and apply. As someone committed to long-term growth, I found the blend of psychology, leadership, and strategy incredibly practical and insightful. Whether you're a student just starting out or a seasoned leader, this is a cornerstone reference you'll keep coming back to."

– DD Mishra,
Thought Leader, Researcher,
Social Worker and Vice President, Gartner

Organizations invest heavily in training, tools, and technology—but often overlook the human side of performance. Burnout, disengagement, and lack of career clarity remain major hurdles.

Dr. Kamaljeet Kaur Siddhu's *"Vaccination for Survival in the Corporate World"* addresses this gap brilliantly. Her holistic approach, combining wellbeing, skill-building, and leadership development, provides a roadmap for professionals to protect and enhance their career longevity.

This book is not just for employees; it is essential reading for anyone responsible for nurturing talent and building high-performing teams.

– Dr.SPRao Borde,
Director - Students Progression and Corporate Relations
Ajeenkya DY Patil Group and Chairman -
Federation of Training and Placement Officers

In today's global business world, uncertainty is the only constant. Managing a company across continents means facing nonstop change, risk and pressure. Success isn't just about what you know - it's about how well you prepare, adapt and stay resilient.

Dr. Kamaljeet Kaur Siddhu presents a powerful, timeless framework in her groundbreaking work, " Vaccination for Survival in the Corporate World". This book equips professional with practical strategies to build career immunity, helping them thrive amid disruption and complexity.

Whether you're an emerging leader or a seasoned executive, this is your ultimate guide to staying strong, adaptable and future - ready in an unpredictable corporate landscape.

– **Sandeep Malhotra,**
Associate Director Sales and Operations - Leading Overseas Education MNC

ACKNOWLEDGMENTS

As I take the step of sharing *"Vaccination for Survival in the Corporate World"* with readers, I feel deeply compelled to acknowledge the incredible individuals whose support and encouragement have made this journey possible.

First and foremost, I extend my heartfelt gratitude to my beloved husband, Kripal Singh Siddhu, whose unwavering love, patience, and encouragement have been my anchor throughout this endeavor. To my wonderful children, Jessica and Montek Singh, thank you for inspiring me daily with your kindness, curiosity, and faith in me.

I am profoundly grateful to my parents, Bishan Singh Real and Dharmi Devi Real, whose wisdom, guidance, and unconditional love have shaped the person I am today. Special thanks to my mother-in-law, Jaya, for her blessings and constant encouragement.

To my sister, Manjeet Kaur Malhotra, your constant support and words of motivation have been invaluable. My heartfelt appreciation also goes to my elder brother, Jagdish Singh Real, and his wife Anuradha, as well as my younger brother, Surjeet Singh Real, and his wife Pinky—each of you has been a pillar of strength, reminding me that I am never alone in this journey.

I would also like to express my gratitude to all my mentors, bosses, and colleagues. Collaborating with you provided experiences, insights, and inspiration that have shaped the ideas in this book. Without your guidance, this project would have taken far longer to come to life.

Special thanks to my Toastmasters friends, Minu Rani and Sanat Deshpande, whose consistent follow-ups and encouragement kept me motivated and on track throughout the publication process.

This book is the result of the love, support, and belief of so many remarkable people. I am eternally thankful to each one of you for helping bring *"Vaccination for Survival in the Corporate World"* into existence.

With deepest gratitude and love,

Dr. Kamaljeet Kaur Siddhu

VACCINATION FOR SURIVAL IN CORPORATE WORLD

A vaccine is a biological preparation that helps your immune system recognize and fight specific diseases. It contains weakened, inactive, or parts of a pathogen (like a virus or bacteria) to "train" your body to build immunity without causing the illness.

Vaccines prevent diseases, reduce their severity, and protect both individuals and communities (herd immunity). They're vital for controlling infectious diseases like polio, measles, and flu, and for tackling newer threats like COVID-19.

By taking the terminologies of biological vaccines I have tried to create "Corporate Survival Vaccines" – each representing a mindset, skill, or habit that will protect employees from "corporate infections" like stress, politics, burnout, or stagnation.

Haha, if only! A "corporate survival vaccine" would be awesome, right? Maybe it'd include doses of resilience, adaptability, teamwork, and a booster shot of stress management with a sprinkle of office politics immunity.

But since science isn't there yet, I suggest that employees should build their own "immunity" through skills like communication, networking, and emotional intelligence. Add a strong dose of self-care and work-life balance, and you're set to thrive in the corporate jungle!

Welcome to the corporate world — a dynamic, fast-paced ecosystem where opportunities, challenges, and competition coexist in equal measure. Just like your body faces threats from viruses, bacteria, and other hazards, your professional journey is exposed to career risks: stress, burnout, office politics, obsolescence, and missed growth opportunities. The difference? Unlike natural immunity, your career immunity is not automatic. It must be cultivated, strengthened, and maintained deliberately.

This book introduces a revolutionary framework: Corporate Survival & Thriving Vaccines, a collection of 30 strategic doses designed to provide full career immunity. Each "vaccine" represents a skill, mindset, or practice that protects you against specific professional risks, while also enhancing your growth, influence, and leadership potential.

Think of it as your personal career immunization program. Some vaccines protect against immediate risks, like managing toxic colleagues or avoiding burnout. Others provide long-term immunity, like strategic thinking, vision, and innovation. Taken together, these doses ensure that you not only survive the corporate ecosystem but thrive in it — building a resilient, sustainable, and fulfilling career.

Why Career Vaccines Are Essential

The corporate world is full of uncertainties:

- **Organizational changes** like mergers, acquisitions, and restructuring can disrupt careers overnight.
- **Technological advancements** can make skills obsolete faster than you think.
- **Interpersonal dynamics** — from office politics to difficult stakeholders — can derail even the most talented professionals.
- **Stress and workload** can burn out even the most dedicated employees.

Without a structured approach to immunity, even high performers risk stagnation, frustration, or irrelevance. The Career Vaccines framework is designed to inoculate against these risks proactively, equipping you with resilience, adaptability, and strategic advantage.

How to Use This Book

1. **Understand Each Vaccine**: Every chapter introduces a "vaccine" — a skill, mindset, or practice that addresses a specific career risk.
2. **Learn Through Stories**: Realistic corporate narratives illustrate how employees have applied these vaccines to thrive.
3. **Apply the Prescription**: Practical, actionable steps accompany each vaccine so you can implement them in your daily work life.

4. **Build Your Immunity Program**: Like a health vaccination schedule, take these doses deliberately and consistently. Over time, you will develop full career **immunity** — the ability to survive challenges, seize opportunities, and advance to executive leadership with confidence.

What Full Career Immunity Looks Like

A professional with full career immunity:

- Thrives under pressure without panic.
- Stays relevant despite technological and market changes.
- Builds strong alliances, networks, and mentorships.
- Handles criticism, conflict, and office politics without stress.
- Inspires trust, loyalty, and influence across teams and stakeholders.
- Maintains personal health, balance, and energy for sustainable performance.
- Sees beyond immediate tasks to think strategically and create long-term impact.

In essence, career immunity is not about luck or avoiding risk; it's about preparation, resilience, and smart action. Just as vaccines protect the body by training it to respond effectively to threats, these 30 corporate vaccines equip you to respond effectively to career challenges and opportunities.

A Personal Invitation

This book is for anyone seeking more than just survival in corporate life — whether you are a new joiner navigating your first job, a mid-level manager aiming for senior leadership, or a seasoned professional aspiring for executive roles. By embracing these 30 doses, you are investing in your most valuable asset: your career longevity and impact.

Prepare to take your first dose, and begin the journey toward full career immunity. Each chapter is your prescription for growth, resilience, and leadership. By the end, you will not just survive the corporate world — you will thrive in it.

The First 10 Career Vaccines – Building Your Core Immunity

The foundation of full career immunity begins with these **10 essential vaccines**. They equip you to face tough projects, master corporate processes, and handle interpersonal challenges — the core ingredients of professional resilience. Each vaccine is a dose of knowledge, mindset, or skill that shields you from early-career pitfalls and sets you on a trajectory for growth.

A. Survival Vaccines (Basic Immunity – Entry Level)

CHAPTER 1

EXPERIENCE VACCINE (LIVE ATTENUATED) – LEARN BY FACING TOUGH PROJECTS.

"Experience Vaccine (Live Attenuated): Learn by Facing Tough Projects"

Just like a live attenuated vaccine uses a weakened form of a virus to build immunity, tough projects and difficult situations "train" you to handle the real pressures of corporate life.

Story – "Riya and the Experience Vaccine"- *The Tough Project That Saved Her Career*

Riya joined a global tech company fresh out of college. Bright, ambitious, and full of energy, she was immediately assigned to a failing internal automation project—one that senior employees had quietly avoided.

At first, Riya felt she'd been set up to fail. Deadlines were unrealistic, the client was frustrated, and her small team was demotivated. But instead of running, she decided this was her "Experience Vaccine."

She began by shadowing her senior for two weeks, asking endless questions, mapping the workflow, and identifying the real blockers—poor communication and unclear ownership. She called short daily stand-ups, created a simple visual tracker, and started celebrating small milestones.

Three months later, the project was back on track. Her manager called her "the quiet storm that turned things around." But what mattered more was what Riya had learned:

- How to manage conflict without authority
- How to simplify chaos
- How to take accountability even when no one asked

Two years later, when a critical client account faced crisis, the leadership team didn't hesitate—they handed it to Riya. She'd already developed the antibodies.

Today, she leads transformation projects across three countries and often tells new joiners,

"Don't look for comfort in your first year. Look for exposure. Every challenge you survive now is a dose of lifelong career immunity."

Prescription for Corporate New Joinees

In the journey of professional growth, no training program or classroom session can match the power of *real-world experience.* The Experience Vaccine (Live Attenuated) is built from exposure — facing the live "viruses" of corporate life: demanding deadlines, complex projects, difficult bosses, and unexpected crises. Each challenge you encounter, survive, and reflect upon strengthens your corporate immunity.

This vaccine doesn't eliminate challenges; it teaches you how to thrive in them. The tougher the project, the stronger your professional antibodies become. Here's how to administer this vaccine effectively:

Dose 1. Say Yes to Stretch Assignments

The most transformative opportunities rarely come neatly packaged within your comfort zone. Growth begins the moment you say "yes" to something that slightly scares you.
Don't wait until you feel fully ready — readiness is a myth. Take on projects that demand new skills, involve new teams, or expose you to higher visibility. These *stretch assignments* simulate leadership far better than theoretical training ever could.
Even if you stumble, remember: every failed attempt injects a dose of resilience, confidence, and humility — the antibodies against fear and self-doubt.

Dose 2. Embrace the Discomfort

Every ambitious professional eventually faces chaos — unclear expectations, shifting priorities, or conflicting feedback. Your instinct might be to retreat, but real leaders lean in.

When things feel messy, treat it as your leadership laboratory. Learn to stay calm amidst confusion and to create clarity where none exists.

No one gets promoted for following instructions; promotions go to those who can *find direction when none is given.* Discomfort is not a signal to stop — it's the environment where true capability is born.

Dose 3. Observe, Then Act

Before you rush into execution, pause to understand the playing field. Study the ecosystem — who truly influences decisions, what defines success in your team, and which rules are written versus implied.

Every organization has a visible hierarchy and an invisible power grid. Learn both.

Observation before action helps you align your efforts with what really matters — this is the difference between being busy and being effective.

Dose 4. Ask, Don't Assume

Many new professionals fear that asking questions will make them look inexperienced. In truth, *smart questions* reflect curiosity, courage, and clarity of thought.

Use every opportunity to learn from seniors, mentors, and even peers. Every experienced professional once faced the same chaos you're experiencing now — they've already built the immunity you seek.
Don't reinvent the wheel; instead, borrow their hard-earned lessons to accelerate your own learning curve.

Dose 5. Document and Reflect

After each project — especially the challenging ones — take time to analyze what happened.

Ask yourself:

- What went right?
- What went wrong?
- What did I learn?
- What will I do differently next time?

This process creates your Career Inoculation Record — a personal growth log that tracks your evolution from novice to seasoned professional. Reflection transforms experience into wisdom.

Dose 6. Manage Ego Exposure

Tough projects often sting — not because of workload, but because they expose our ego. You may receive criticism, face rejection, or be proven wrong.

This is where your immunity is truly tested. Stay teachable. Listen more, defend less.

Immunity doesn't come from always being right; it comes from staying open, humble, and adaptable in moments when your ego wants to fight back.

Dose 7. Develop Cross-Functional Muscles

Success in modern organizations depends on collaboration across departments. Volunteer for inter-departmental projects — they stretch your thinking and expose you to how the business actually runs.

Understanding multiple systems — finance, operations, marketing, HR — makes you far less likely to be blindsided later.

Each new collaboration is like a booster dose, strengthening your adaptability and organizational intelligence.

Dose 8. Celebrate Micro-Wins

Building immunity is not an overnight transformation; it's a gradual strengthening process. Celebrate every small victory — presenting confidently in a tough meeting, resolving a conflict, meeting a tight deadline, or saving a faltering project.

These micro-wins are signs that your antibodies are working. Acknowledge them, reflect on them, and let them motivate you to take on even bigger challenges.

Final Dose: Live the Experience, Don't Fear It

The **Experience Vaccine** works only when faced live — in real-time challenges that test your patience, problem-solving, and emotional balance. Each experience, good or bad, adds a new layer of protection against future uncertainty.

So, when your next tough project comes along, don't duck for cover — step forward with courage. Every challenge is not an obstacle; it's an *immunity booster in disguise.*

Thus, **Tough projects are not punishments—they are vaccinations against future burnout, fear, and stagnation.**

Take the shot. Build your immunity. Thrive for life.

CHAPTER 2

PROCESS VACCINE (INACTIVATED) – MASTER POLICIES, COMPLIANCE, SOPS.

For lasting career immunity — learn the rules before you rewrite them.

Just as an inactivated vaccine uses a harmless form of a virus to build resistance, mastering your company's *policies, processes, and SOPs* (Standard Operating Procedures) protects you from hidden career risks — compliance issues, procedural delays, or ethical missteps.

Story: "Rohan and the Process Vaccine": *The Rulebook That Saved His Reputation*

Rohan was a management trainee in a large FMCG firm — bright, fast-talking, and ambitious. In his first month, he found the company's processes tedious: daily reports, approval matrices, travel logs, and compliance forms.

While others slogged through SOPs, Rohan prided himself on "getting things done quickly." One day, during a regional campaign, he hired a vendor without the required three quotations — a shortcut he thought was harmless. The campaign succeeded, but Finance flagged his payment as *non-compliant.*

An internal review began. Though Rohan hadn't done anything unethical, he couldn't produce documentation proving due diligence. The project's success was overshadowed by a procedural lapse.

That's when his mentor stepped in:

"Rohan, results make you visible, but processes make you sustainable. Learn both."

Humbled, Rohan spent the next three months shadowing the operations team. He studied how approvals, audits, and policy frameworks worked. He built his own mini "process map" for every task he handled.

Soon, colleagues started coming to him for clarity on procurement and compliance rules. His boss nicknamed him *"Mr. SOP."*

A year later, when the company launched a new division, Rohan was asked to design its operating framework — because he understood both *speed and structure.*

Today, Rohan laughs,

"The rulebook I once ignored became my strongest career vaccine. It didn't slow me down — it kept me safe enough to run faster."

Prescription for Corporate New Joinees Process Vaccine (Inactivated) – Master policies, compliance, SOPs.

In the world of corporate survival, even the most talented professionals falter when they ignore one crucial element — the system itself. Every organization has its own *immune system* made up of policies, processes, and compliance mechanisms. While these may appear rigid or bureaucratic at first glance, they are, in fact, the invisible infrastructure that keeps operations efficient, fair, and legally sound.

The *Process Vaccine (Inactivated)* prepares new joinees to understand, respect, and skillfully navigate this structure. It doesn't kill creativity — it channels it through the right pathways. Once you master the processes, you don't just fit into the organization; you flow through it with confidence and credibility.

Dose 1. Decode the DNA of Your Organization

Before you start innovating, start observing. Every company has its unique rhythm — its DNA. Understand how work actually flows: who approves what, how decisions are documented, and which tools are used for communication and record-keeping.

Spend time exploring your company's intranet, process manuals, policy dashboards, and internal systems. Learn the acronyms, the templates, and the unofficial shortcuts that are still within the rules.

Knowing *who to ask* and *what form to use* saves you from delays, friction, and unnecessary escalations. The ability to decode the process early is the difference between chaos and clarity.

Dose 2. Compliance is Confidence

Many bright professionals damage their reputation by ignoring small formalities — missing report deadlines, mishandling confidential data, or submitting expense claims casually. What seems like minor negligence signals a lack of discipline and reliability.

Compliance is not about blind obedience — it's about respect for the ecosystem you're part of. Following systems precisely doesn't make you rigid; it makes you dependable.

In fact, *compliance builds confidence* — in your managers, your team, and your own professional identity.

Dose 3. Don't Shortcut the System — Learn to Navigate It

The fastest path in the corporate maze is not to break the rules but to understand them so thoroughly that you can move through them with ease.

Shortcuts might offer temporary speed, but they come at the cost of long-term credibility. Instead, become the employee who knows how things get done *the right way*.

Process mastery doesn't slow you down — it streamlines you. When you know which doors to knock and in what sequence, you get approvals faster, avoid rework, and earn the trust of your stakeholders.

Dose 4. Master Documentation Early

In the corporate world, memory fades — but documentation remains.

Keep written records of key decisions, feedback, and approvals. Whether it's an email confirmation or a formal note, good documentation protects you from misunderstandings and serves as evidence of due diligence.

Think of documentation as your professional insurance — it doesn't just protect you; it also helps you clarify your own thought process.

Dose 5. Know the Non-Negotiables

Every organization has boundaries that cannot be crossed. These come in the form of HR, Finance, Legal, and IT policies.

Understanding these rules is not optional — it's your personal and professional shield. Learn the essentials:

- Leave policies and reporting protocols
- Data privacy and cybersecurity norms
- Non-Disclosure Agreements (NDAs)
- Conflict of interest guidelines

These policies are not obstacles; they're the *immune barriers* that safeguard both you and the company from reputational or legal harm.

Dose 6. Build Your SOP Library

The smartest professionals create their own "Process Bible."

Start by maintaining a personal collection of one-page guides or checklists for your recurring tasks — be it project initiation, client updates, or budget submissions.

This personalized library becomes your booster shot during high-pressure times. It prevents errors, ensures consistency, and frees your mental bandwidth for creative problem-solving.

Dose 7. Be the 'Go-To' Person for Process Clarity

In every workplace, there's someone people turn to when they're unsure about how to get things done — *be that person.*

When colleagues and managers recognize you as someone who knows the system, they trust you with more responsibility.

Leaders value employees who combine creativity with compliance. Reliability in process is often the unseen ladder that leads to leadership.

Dose 8. Update Yourself — Stay Immunized

Policies evolve as organizations grow. What was acceptable last year might be obsolete today. Keep your process knowledge current — subscribe to internal newsletters, policy updates, and compliance notifications.

Just like vaccines need boosters, your process immunity requires regular refreshers. Staying updated ensures you never fall behind on the organization's rhythm.

Final Dose:

The *Process Vaccine* may not sound glamorous, but it's one of the most powerful. It transforms you from a newcomer to a confident insider who knows how to get things done without chaos or confusion. Once you master the system, the system begins to work *for you*, not *against you.*

Mastering processes is not about rigidity — it's about reliability.

Systems don't limit creativity; they *liberate* it by creating a safe space for excellence.

The Process Vaccine makes you trusted, consistent, and immune to career breakdowns.

CHAPTER 3

MINDSET VACCINE (MRNA) – ADAPT, LEARN, UNLEARN

For long-term corporate survival, evolve faster than your environment.

Just as an mRNA vaccine trains the body to recognize and respond to new variants, a growth mindset trains professionals to stay relevant, resilient, and ready — no matter how fast the corporate world mutates.

Story: "Meera and the Mindset Vaccine"- *The Analyst Who Became a Strategist*

Meera joined a leading financial firm as a data analyst. In her first year, she was meticulous and precise — but also rigid. She followed the same spreadsheet routines daily, confident that consistency was her strength.

Then came a disruption: her company adopted a new AI-based analytics system. Overnight, her old processes became irrelevant. Many peers grumbled, but Meera remembered her mentor's words:

"In this company, immunity comes from agility."

Instead of resisting, she enrolled in free online AI and visualization courses. She started experimenting after hours, applying new insights to automate her team's weekly reports. Within months, her dashboards reduced manual work by 60%.

When the leadership team noticed, they invited her to co-lead a cross-functional project on digital transformation — something far beyond her original role.

Three years later, Meera no longer just analyzes data — she *designs strategies* for how the firm uses it. Her motto is simple:

"Every few months, I ask myself — what version of me is outdated? And then, I upgrade."

She didn't just survive the change; she became *the change.*

Prescription for Corporate New Joinees to Build the Mindset Vaccine

In the rapidly shifting corporate world, the most valuable skill is not just knowledge — it's *adaptability.* The "Mindset Vaccine" prepares you to think, learn, and grow continuously so that you don't just survive change — you thrive on it. Every organization evolves, technologies disrupt, and priorities shift. Those who can recalibrate their mindset without resistance become indispensable. This chapter offers a practical prescription for developing a mindset that's immune to fear, fixed thinking, and stagnation.

Dose 1. Adapt Faster Than You Judge

The first reaction to change is often judgment — "Why are we doing this?" or "This won't work." But judgment blocks understanding.

Instead, learn to interpret change before resisting it. Every corporate shift — whether it's a new manager, policy, or project — brings hidden opportunities to showcase your adaptability.

Ask yourself: *What's the new value I can add in this scenario?*

When you pivot faster than you panic, you not only stay relevant — you stand out. The most adaptable employees naturally evolve into leaders because they model resilience and flexibility for others.

Dose 2. Keep Your Learning Muscles Active

Learning in the corporate world isn't an event — it's a lifestyle.

Treat every project, meeting, and even mistake as a masterclass. Every time you take on a new responsibility, approach it like a student — curious, humble, and eager to grow.

Set a personal rule: learn one new tool, concept, or process each month, even if it doesn't directly relate to your role. The corporate ecosystem rewards the curious generalist as much as the expert specialist.

Over time, your continuous learning habit becomes your strongest career antibody.

Dose 3. Unlearn Comfortably

Often, success in one context becomes the obstacle in another. What helped you succeed in college or a past job may not work in your new environment.

Unlearning is the art of releasing outdated habits, methods, and mindsets. It's harder than learning because it requires humility — admitting that what once worked may no longer serve you.

Ask yourself periodically: *Which belief or habit might be outdated now?*

When you learn to unlearn gracefully, you remain fluid, future-ready, and open to transformation.

Dose 4. Seek Feedback Fearlessly

Feedback is not a verdict — it's data.

In the early stages of your corporate career, feedback is your fastest route to improvement. Ask for it frequently, receive it gracefully, and act on it visibly.

Even if feedback stings, remember — it's rarely about your worth as a person, but about how you can refine your performance.

By treating feedback as "real-time performance research," you turn criticism into clarity and growth into a measurable, ongoing process.

Dose 5. Build Digital Agility

Technology evolves faster than most job titles. A key part of a resilient mindset is digital agility — the confidence and curiosity to explore new tools before you're forced to use them.

Be the first to experiment with emerging software, dashboards, and AI tools in your workplace.

Digital fluency has become the modern mRNA strand of corporate immunity — the more agile you are digitally, the more indispensable you become.

Dose 6. Be Curious, Not Cynical

Cynicism is the easiest trap for intelligent professionals. It feels smart to say, "This won't work." But curiosity asks, "How might this work better?"

When new strategies, leaders, or colleagues enter the picture, start by asking questions — not making conclusions. Curiosity keeps your creative neurons firing and your professional antibodies strong.

A curious mind remains in motion, while a cynical one gets stuck in its own skepticism.

Dose 7. Create Micro-Pivots

Careers don't need massive overhauls — they need micro-adjustments.

Every six to twelve months, conduct a personal growth audit:

- Which of my skills are becoming outdated?

- What new tools or competencies are in demand?
- What roles or opportunities excite me now?

These small, regular pivots keep you evolving naturally, so you're never caught unprepared when industries change. Reinvent yourself proactively — before the market forces you to.

Dose 8. Surround Yourself with Lifelong Learners

Your mindset is shaped by the company you keep. Energy is contagious — and so is stagnation.

Seek out mentors, colleagues, and friends who challenge your thinking, recommend insightful books or courses, and celebrate growth.

When you engage with learners, you absorb their drive; when you associate with complainers, you inherit their limits.

Choose your professional ecosystem consciously — because your network influences your next move more than you realize.

Final Dose:

Your *Mindset Vaccine* is not a one-time shot — it's a lifelong booster. The moment you stop learning, you start decaying. In an age where industries reinvent themselves every few years, the ability to adapt, unlearn, and grow is your ultimate immunity.

The Mindset Vaccine protects you from professional extinction.

Adaptation is not a reaction — it's a readiness.

The faster you learn, unlearn, and relearn, the stronger your career immunity becomes.

CHAPTER 4

RELATIONSHIP VACCINE (CONJUGATE) – BUILD AUTHENTIC ALLIANCES AND NETWORKS

Because immunity in the corporate world is collective, not individual.

Just like a **conjugate vaccine** links a weak antigen to a strong carrier to boost the immune response, your professional strength multiplies when you connect your skills with strong, authentic relationships.

In the corporate ecosystem, your *network is your antibody reservoir.*

Story: "Arjun and the Relationship Vaccine" - *The Network That Saved His Career*

Arjun joined a top consulting firm as a junior associate. Brilliant with numbers but introverted by nature, he preferred working quietly on his laptop rather than engaging with colleagues.

When a restructuring hit his department, several roles were merged — including his. While others found new positions through internal recommendations, Arjun had no strong allies. For the first time, he realized that technical excellence wasn't enough; *relationships were resilience.*

Determined to change, Arjun began small — volunteering to help on cross-team projects, attending internal learning sessions, and offering to review juniors' presentations. He made it a point to thank others publicly for their collaboration.

Over time, people began noticing his supportive attitude. His reputation shifted from "quiet analyst" to "reliable team player."

A year later, when a high-visibility transformation project began, a senior partner — whom Arjun had once helped on a late-night report — personally recommended him for the core team.

That project became Arjun's career breakthrough.

Today, when he mentors new employees, he says:

"Skills make you employable. Relationships make you unshakable."

His immunity wasn't built from power — it was built from connection.

Prescription for Corporate New Joinees to Build the Relationship Vaccine

"In the corporate world, it's not just what you know — it's how you connect that determines how far you go."

When you step into a new corporate environment, you carry your qualifications, your enthusiasm, and your ambition. But there's another invisible asset that determines your success — **relationships**.

Relationships are the arteries through which trust, collaboration, and opportunity flow. They form the emotional infrastructure of every organization. A well-built relationship network doesn't just help you grow faster — it also cushions you during challenges, misunderstandings, and change.

To thrive in any organization, new joinees must develop the **Relationship Vaccine** — a set of practices that build genuine connections, mutual respect, and long-term professional goodwill.

Here's your **prescription** to build lasting relational immunity.

Dose 1: Earn Trust Before You Need It

Trust is the foundation of every healthy professional relationship — and like fitness, it must be built consistently before it's tested.

Don't wait for a crisis, project deadline, or personal favor to start nurturing relationships.

- Be reliable in your commitments — do what you promise.
- Communicate with empathy and honesty.
- Follow through on even small tasks.

Trust is built in **droplets** — through small, daily actions of dependability — but it can be lost in **buckets** through one careless act of disrespect or negligence.

Protect it like a precious asset, because that's exactly what it is.

Dose 2: Connect Beyond Job Titles

True professionalism is measured not by how you treat your seniors, but by how you treat everyone around you.

From security guards to housekeeping staff, admin teams, and support departments — every person adds value to the organization's ecosystem.

A simple greeting, a thank-you note, or an acknowledgment of someone's contribution can make a profound impact.

The most respected leaders are not those who command authority — they are those who **extend respect universally**.

Treat everyone with equal dignity, and you'll build a reputation that travels faster than your designation.

Dose 3: Seek Mentors, Not Favourites

As a new joinee, you'll naturally look for guidance. But remember — a good mentor doesn't flatter; they **stretch** you.

- Identify people who challenge your thinking, question your assumptions, and push you toward growth.
- Seek feedback from those who've walked the path before you.
- Don't wait for a formal mentorship program — mentorship often starts with one good question and genuine curiosity.

A good mentor is a **mirror**, reflecting your blind spots and potential — not a megaphone echoing your comfort zone.

Dose 4: Give Before You Get

Healthy relationships thrive on reciprocity, not transaction.

Share knowledge, resources, and appreciation freely, even when there's nothing immediate to gain.

When you help others succeed — by sharing insights, volunteering assistance, or celebrating their wins — you weave an invisible network of goodwill.

In times of uncertainty or challenge, that goodwill becomes your **safety net**.

Remember: people remember those who helped them rise, not those who competed to shine.

Dose 5: Learn the Art of Stakeholder Balance

Every project, no matter how small, involves different personalities — the **supportive**, the **skeptical**, and the **silent**.

Mapping your stakeholders early helps you communicate with wisdom rather than frustration.

- Supportive people need acknowledgment and updates.
- Skeptical ones need data and reassurance.
- Silent stakeholders often hold quiet influence — earn their trust with respect and inclusion.

Balancing these relationships is not politics — it's emotional intelligence in action. It's how successful professionals sustain harmony without losing authenticity.

Dose 6: Handle Conflict with Grace

Disagreements are inevitable in any workplace. What defines your maturity is how you handle them.

Don't personalize conflicts or convert them into ego battles.

Focus on **resolving issues, not winning arguments**.

Use calm communication, active listening, and empathy to bridge differences.

Emotional maturity is a critical form of **career immunity** — it prevents one moment of anger from undoing years of credibility.

Dose 7: Stay Visible, Not Loud

Visibility is about being recognized for your contributions, not for your volume.

- Participate in discussions, share ideas thoughtfully, and express gratitude publicly.
- Celebrate team achievements rather than personal victories.
- Let your work speak, but also let your presence be felt through consistency and sincerity.

Remember — authenticity always outweighs performance.

Be known for your integrity, not your noise.

Dose 8: Nurture Relationships Long-Term

Relationships don't end when you switch teams or companies; they evolve.

Stay in touch with former colleagues, mentors, and managers.

A five-minute check-in message, a quick congratulations, or sharing a helpful article — these small gestures keep your professional network alive and meaningful.

Sometimes, a door opens years later through a relationship you nurtured with kindness and respect.

That's the beauty of genuine connection — it compounds with time.

Final Dose: Build Bridges, Not Walls

The Relationship Vaccine protects you from corporate isolation and strengthens your professional immunity with empathy, trust, and respect.

When you focus on building bridges — between teams, functions, and personalities — you not only grow your influence but also elevate the culture around you.

In the long run, people won't just remember what you achieved — they'll remember how you made them feel.

And that, more than any performance review, is what creates a lasting legacy in the corporate world.

Relationships are the strongest antibodies in your career.

The corporate world isn't a battlefield; it's an ecosystem.

Those who collaborate, care, and connect don't just survive — they sustain and grow with collective immunity.

CHAPTER 5

EGO-NEUTRALIZER VACCINE (TOXOID) – HANDLE TOXIC PEOPLE WITHOUT ABSORBING NEGATIVITY

Because career immunity is not just about what you learn — it's about what you refuse to let infect you.

Just as a **toxoid vaccine** uses a harmless form of a toxin to train the body to resist real poisons, this vaccine helps you **build inner emotional resilience** against toxic people, office politics, and ego clashes — without losing your calm, confidence, or compassion.

Story: "Nisha and the Ego-Neutralizer Vaccine"- *The Calm That Outlasted the Chaos*

Nisha joined a reputed multinational as a marketing associate — bright, enthusiastic, and full of ideas. Her immediate supervisor, however, was known for being volatile and hyper-critical.

In meetings, he often dismissed her suggestions or took credit for her work. Initially, Nisha felt crushed. She considered quitting — but then she realized this was her test, her "Ego-Neutralizer Vaccine" moment.

Instead of reacting emotionally, she started *responding strategically.*

She began documenting her contributions, communicating updates in writing, and staying unfailingly professional. When criticized, she would calmly say,

"Thank you for the feedback — I'll review it and improve."

Gradually, her calmness became her strength. While others argued, she stayed focused on delivery. Her projects began showing strong results, earning recognition from senior management.

One day, her manager publicly took credit again — but this time, the department head intervened:

"Actually, this initiative was led by Nisha. Her consistent work speaks for itself."

The moment was quiet but powerful. Nisha didn't fight for validation — her integrity earned it.

Years later, as a manager herself, she tells her team:

"You can't stop people from being toxic, but you can stop yourself from being reactive. That's real immunity."

Her emotional maturity became her leadership trademark.

Prescription for Corporate New Joinees to Build the Ego-Neutralizer Vaccine

"In the corporate jungle, it's not the loudest roar that wins — it's the calmest mind."

Every workplace has its share of challenges — not all of them are technical or task-related. Some are emotional and interpersonal. You might encounter colleagues who criticize more than they contribute, gossip more than they guide, or manipulate situations for personal gain.

Such interactions can slowly drain your confidence, distort your focus, and erode your peace — unless you build the **Ego-Neutralizer Vaccine**: a set of mental and emotional habits that keep your calm intact while navigating corporate toxicity.

This vaccine doesn't just protect you from others' egos — it helps you manage your own, ensuring you remain grounded, graceful, and growth-oriented.

Here's your **prescription** for corporate emotional immunity.

Dose 1: Recognize the Toxin Early

The first step to protecting yourself is awareness.

Toxic individuals often reveal themselves through consistent patterns — constant criticism, unnecessary competition, gossip, or manipulation disguised as "feedback."

Don't normalize such behavior. Identify the signs early and create emotional distance.

You can't control who enters your professional space, but you can control how deeply they influence your mental space.

Recognizing the toxin early helps you act with clarity rather than react with emotion.

Dose 2: Don't Absorb — Observe

Not every storm deserves your energy. When confronted with negativity, learn to **observe instead of absorb.**

Visualize yourself as a mirror — reflect back calmness, but don't internalize the drama.

- Listen without reacting emotionally.
- Respond to facts, not feelings.
- Keep your tone steady and professional.

When you shift from emotional engagement to mindful observation, you stop feeding toxicity and start reclaiming control.

Dose 3: Protect Your Energy, Not Your Ego

Toxic behavior often targets your self-worth — with criticism, sarcasm, or subtle put-downs designed to provoke you.

Remember this simple truth:

You don't have to attend every argument you're invited to.

Protect your peace like it's your password — never share it freely.

Instead of defending your ego, defend your energy.

Calm is not weakness; it's quiet power.

Dose 4: Stay Professional, Stay Polite

When someone tries to draw you into an ego battle, resist the urge to respond in kind.

Don't fight ego with ego — it only doubles the damage.

Maintain professionalism, courtesy, and calm composure.

- Speak less, but with purpose.
- Let your body language express dignity, not defiance.
- Remember, silence — when intentional and graceful — can be the most powerful response.

Your restraint speaks volumes about your maturity and emotional intelligence.

Dose 5: Set Clear Boundaries

Boundaries are not about building walls; they're about protecting your inner climate.

Be assertive about your limits — whether it's how people speak to you, how much time you give, or what behavior you tolerate.

Communicate calmly and clearly when something crosses the line.

Healthy boundaries filter out disrespect and make space for respect to thrive.

Boundaries are your self-respect in visible form.

Dose 6: Find Your "Positivity Tribe"

No vaccine works in isolation. Your emotional immunity strengthens when you surround yourself with positive energy.

Seek out **mentors, well-wishers, and colleagues** who uplift, inspire, and challenge you constructively.

Their presence helps you rebalance after a toxic encounter and reminds you of your strengths.

When negativity tries to infiltrate your day, let your positivity tribe act as your emotional firewall.

Dose 7: Reframe Criticism into Clarity

Even in the harshest criticism, there may be a grain of truth — a signal hidden inside the noise.

Extract that truth, discard the venom, and use the insight for self-improvement.

That's emotional alchemy — turning poison into protection.

By reframing criticism as data rather than drama, you keep learning without letting ego get in the way.

Dose 8: Don't Become What You Fight

Repeated exposure to toxic behavior can harden even the kindest people.

Beware of becoming cynical, defensive, or bitter — that's how toxicity spreads.

Protect your compassion. Keep your empathy alive.

Your kindness is not naivety; it's your strongest antidote.

Staying kind in an unkind environment is not weakness — it's mastery.

Final Dose: Choose Calm Over Chaos

The Ego-Neutralizer Vaccine empowers you to remain steady amidst storms, kind amidst conflict, and clear amidst confusion.

You may not always control the energy around you — but you can always control the energy within you.

When you stop reacting to every ego battle and start responding with awareness, you rise above the noise.

You lead with grace. You live with peace.

And that's the ultimate sign of corporate maturity — **strength without aggression, confidence without arrogance, and success without ego.**

You can't detoxify the world, but you can strengthen your inner filter.

The Ego-Neutralizer Vaccine protects your peace, professionalism, and purpose.

It helps you rise above pettiness — and stay focused on progress.

CHAPTER 6

NETWORKING VACCINE (SUBUNIT) – BUILD PROFESSIONAL ALLIANCES EARLY.

Because careers don't grow in isolation — they grow in connection.

Just like a **subunit vaccine** uses selected protein parts of a virus to trigger immunity safely and effectively, *networking strategically* — not superficially — exposes you to diverse professional ideas and people, without overexposure or noise.

Early alliances, when built authentically, create a safety net that sustains your career through every challenge.

Story: "Dev and the Networking Vaccine"-*The Connections That Carried Him Forward*

Dev joined a large manufacturing firm as a graduate trainee. He was smart and sincere but also introverted, preferring solo work over small talk.

During onboarding, he overheard a senior manager say:

"In this company, what you know gets you in the door — but who knows you keeps you there."

The sentence struck him. Dev decided to experiment with networking — his own "subunit vaccine."

He started small: greeting people in the cafeteria, joining internal hobby groups, and asking seniors about their project journeys. He also volunteered to help HR with employee engagement activities — not glamorous work, but it allowed him to meet colleagues across departments.

Soon, when a critical product launch team was being formed, Dev's name surfaced in discussions. A senior manager remembered him from an earlier project meeting and said,

"He's proactive and dependable — let's bring him in."

That opportunity accelerated his learning curve dramatically.

A few years later, when Dev decided to move into a new function, he didn't apply cold — he reached out to a mentor he'd built rapport with. That mentor guided him, endorsed him internally, and ensured he landed the new role smoothly.

Today, Dev mentors new joiners, often saying:

"Networking isn't about collecting contacts. It's about cultivating context. People remember how you made them feel — not what you asked for."

His quiet consistency built him a strong professional web — one that kept catching opportunities before they fell through.

Prescription for Corporate New Joinees to Build the Networking Vaccine

"Your network is your net worth — but only if you nurture it before you need it."

In the modern corporate world, skills and knowledge may get you in the door — but relationships often determine how far you go inside. Networking is not about collecting business cards or followers; it's about cultivating genuine human connections that help you learn, grow, and contribute meaningfully.

Just as our bodies need social and emotional immunity to stay healthy, our careers need **Networking Immunity** — a well-nurtured circle of trust, mentorship, and mutual support.

Here's your **prescription** for building the Networking Vaccine — a set of practices that strengthen your professional relationships from day one.

Dose 1: Start Networking Before You Need It

One of the biggest mistakes young professionals make is waiting for a crisis — a job loss, conflict, or stagnation — to start building connections. By then, it's often too late.

Healthy networks, like strong immune systems, are built **proactively**, not reactively.

- Begin early by engaging with peers, seniors, and colleagues from other departments.
- Participate in conversations, seek perspectives, and learn about what others do.
- Approach people with curiosity, not desperation — genuine interest creates bonds that last.

Your future self will thank you for every connection made with authenticity today.

Dose 2: Be Genuinely Interested, Not Opportunistic

Networking is about **relationships**, not transactions. People can sense when you're reaching out only for favors or opportunities.

Shift your focus from "What can I get?" to "What can I learn or share?"

- Ask about people's experiences, lessons, and stories — not just their titles.
- Remember small details — a colleague's project, hobby, or professional milestone.
- Express appreciation sincerely.

Sincerity builds trust, and trust is the true currency of professional life.

Dose 3: Diversify Your Network

A resilient network is like a well-balanced portfolio — diverse, dynamic, and wide-reaching.

Don't limit yourself to people who do what you do.

- Connect with professionals across departments, functions, and even industries.
- Include people from different age groups, backgrounds, and geographies.
- Exposure to diverse ideas strengthens creativity and gives you access to opportunities you might never have imagined.

When the market shifts, it's your **diverse network** that cushions you and opens new doors.

Dose 4: Show Up and Speak Up

Visibility precedes opportunity. To be remembered, you must be **seen and heard**.

- Attend town halls, training programs, webinars, and social gatherings within your organization.
- Volunteer for cross-functional projects, internal committees, or CSR activities.
- Share your perspectives thoughtfully during discussions — silence might keep you safe, but participation makes you visible.

Every event is a potential connection point; every interaction is a chance to build familiarity.

Dose 5: Add Value First

The strongest relationships are built not on taking, but on **giving**.

Find small ways to contribute:

- Share insightful articles or tools relevant to your colleagues' work.
- Offer feedback or review someone's presentation deck.
- Celebrate their achievements or encourage them during challenging phases.

Even a small act of helpfulness strengthens goodwill. Remember, when you add value first, opportunities find their way back to you — often when you least expect them.

Dose 6: Maintain Your Network

Connections fade without maintenance — just like muscles weaken without exercise.

Keep your relationships alive with small, consistent gestures:

- Send a short check-in message every few months.
- Congratulate people on promotions, new roles, or professional milestones.
- Share a relevant article or update that might interest them.

These simple acts show that you care — and caring is what keeps your network beating with life.

Dose 7: Use Digital Presence Wisely

In today's world, your **online presence** speaks before you do. Make it count.

- Keep your LinkedIn profile updated with your achievements, learnings, and reflections.

- Engage meaningfully — comment on posts, share insights, and highlight others' good work.
- Maintain professionalism and positivity in your digital footprint.

Your online visibility should reinforce your offline reputation — thoughtful, trustworthy, and growth-oriented.

Dose 8: Turn Mentors into Multipliers

Mentorship is a two-way street. Great mentors guide you only if you respect their time and demonstrate your effort.

- Seek guidance genuinely, not just for advice but for learning from their journey.
- More importantly, update them on how you applied their suggestions.
- When mentors see you implementing feedback, they invest more deeply in your growth.

A mentor who feels valued becomes a **multiplier** — someone who not only teaches you but also connects you to new circles of influence.

Dose 9: Be the Connector

True networking mastery comes when you start connecting others, not just yourself.

- Introduce people who could benefit from knowing each other — colleagues, vendors, or partners.
- Celebrate others' strengths publicly.

- When you bridge opportunities for others, you gain trust and respect across both ends.

The connector earns a **priceless reputation** — as someone who empowers, not competes. And in the long run, that's what defines leadership.

Final Dose: Build Relationships, Not Contacts

Networking is not a sprint; it's a lifelong marathon. It thrives on mutual respect, consistency, and empathy.

When you treat every interaction as an opportunity to **build trust, exchange value, and learn something new**, you're not just growing your network — you're strengthening your professional immunity against isolation, stagnation, and burnout.

Stay curious about people. Stay generous with connections.

Because in the end, the most powerful vaccine for career growth isn't just *who you know* — it's *how you nurture who you know.*

Your network is your career's immune system.

Build it before you need it, nurture it with authenticity, and protect it with integrity.

The Networking Vaccine doesn't just open doors — it ensures they never close completely.

CHAPTER 7

SKILL-UPGRADATION VACCINE (MRNA) – STAY RELEVANT THROUGH CONSTANT LEARNING.

The only permanent skill in the corporate world is the ability to keep learning.

Just like the **mRNA vaccine** trains your body to respond to new variants, this "career vaccine" trains your mind to **anticipate change, re-skill quickly, and thrive in evolving environments.**

The faster you learn, the longer you stay immune to career stagnation.

Story: "Ananya and the Skill-Upgradation Vaccine"- *The Analyst Who Rebooted Her Career*

Ananya joined a leading logistics company right after her MBA. Smart, hardworking, and detail-oriented, she quickly mastered reporting and analytics in Excel and PowerPoint. For the first two years, she was the "go-to" person for monthly dashboards and performance metrics.

But soon, a quiet disruption began.

The company's new digital transformation strategy introduced AI-powered analytics and automation tools. Reports that once took Ananya three days could now be generated in thirty seconds.

Suddenly, her once-coveted skills were becoming outdated.

Her younger colleagues were already experimenting with Power BI, Python, and machine learning dashboards. Ananya felt anxious — she feared becoming invisible in the very organization she'd helped streamline.

One day, during a feedback session, her manager gently said,

"You're capable and disciplined, Ananya. But your skillset needs a version upgrade. The world won't wait for us to catch up."

That evening, she made a decision: she would not let comfort become her career's slow poison.

She enrolled in an online certification in data visualization. Every night after work, she spent two hours learning new tools. She began automating small parts of her own reports, testing scripts, and creating interactive dashboards.

When she hit roadblocks, she reached out to IT colleagues for tips — learning informally, but consistently.

Six months later, she presented a pilot project that used real-time tracking and predictive analytics for shipment delays. It impressed the senior leadership so much that they asked her to lead a cross-department task force for analytics transformation.

Two years later, Ananya wasn't just an analyst anymore — she became the **Head of Data Insights.**

During a company town hall, she shared her journey and said:

"I realized that professional extinction begins the moment you stop learning.

Every new skill is a vaccine against obsolescence."

Her story became a case study for the company's induction program — proof that when you treat learning as a habit, not a hobby, your career never expires.

Prescription for Corporate New Joinees for Skill-Upgradation Vaccine (mRNA) – Stay relevant through constant learning.

"In a rapidly changing corporate world, your greatest asset isn't what you know today—it's how fast you can learn tomorrow."

The workplace is evolving faster than ever — new technologies, shifting business models, and changing expectations are rewriting what it means to be "qualified." In this dynamic environment, the most powerful vaccine you can take as a corporate professional — especially as a new joinee — is the **Skill-Upgradation Vaccine**.

This vaccine doesn't come in a syringe; it comes through **continuous learning, adaptability**, and a commitment to stay relevant. Here's your 10-dose prescription to build it.

Dose 1: Adopt the "Always-in-Beta" Mindset

Think of yourself as a **product in development** — always improving, refining, and upgrading. Just like apps release new versions to stay competitive, you must too.

Every year, pause and ask yourself:

"What version of myself do I need to become next?"

Being "Always-in-Beta" keeps you agile, open to feedback, and fearless in the face of change. Remember: progress, not perfection, is the true hallmark of growth.

Dose 2: Build a Personal Learning Plan

Learning doesn't happen by accident; it happens by design. Create a **personal learning roadmap** that aligns with where your industry is heading.

- Identify **2–3 skills** that are future-critical — whether in digital literacy, leadership, communication, or domain depth.
- Dedicate fixed, non-negotiable time for growth. Even **30 minutes a day** adds up to nearly **180 hours a year** — enough to transform your capabilities.

Learning is an investment that compounds with time — and the earlier you start, the richer the dividends.

Dose 3: Learn Beyond Your Job Description

Don't confine yourself to your role boundaries. The most successful professionals are those who understand how the entire business functions.

Explore how other teams — finance, marketing, operations, HR, or tech — contribute to the organization's success.

This **cross-functional awareness** gives you the versatility and strategic vision that leaders are known for.

Dose 4: Micro-Learn Every Day

In a world of information overload, the secret is **micro-learning** — small, daily doses of new knowledge.

- Watch a short explainer video.
- Read a thought-provoking article.
- Listen to a 10-minute podcast on your commute.

Learning isn't about courses and certificates anymore; it's about nurturing **curiosity as a daily reflex.**

Dose 5: Apply, Don't Just Accumulate

Learning without application is like a vaccine that's never activated.

Test your new knowledge immediately — join a pilot project, volunteer for an initiative, or propose an improvement in your team's workflow.

Application turns theory into wisdom and helps you stand out as someone who doesn't just *learn*, but *implements.*

Dose 6: Stay Tech-Agile

Technology is no longer an IT department's responsibility — it's everyone's.

Regardless of your field, being **digitally fluent** is the new corporate language.

Explore tools related to AI, data analysis, project automation, and digital communication. Learn how to use them, not fear them.

In tomorrow's world, **those who understand tech will lead those who don't.**

Dose 7: Seek Feedback as a Learning Trigger

Every piece of feedback is a **free training session** — customized for you.

Don't wait for annual reviews; proactively seek feedback from peers, mentors, and leaders.

Treat every comment as a data point that helps you debug your performance and improve your "next version."

The fastest learners are those who listen, reflect, and recalibrate quickly.

Dose 8: Find Your Learning Tribe

Growth is contagious when shared. Surround yourself with people who challenge, inspire, and uplift you.

Form or join **learning circles**, reading groups, or cross-team discussions where new ideas are exchanged freely.

A strong learning ecosystem fuels collective progress — and your motivation thrives when others are learning alongside you.

Dose 9: Teach to Reinforce

When you teach, you don't just share knowledge — you strengthen your own mastery.

Conduct mini-workshops, share insights on LinkedIn, or mentor a junior colleague.

Teaching makes you visible as a **knowledge leader**, builds confidence, and keeps you engaged in continuous self-improvement.

Dose 10: Celebrate Curiosity, Not Just Competence

Perfection is temporary; curiosity is timeless.

Stay open to questions, ideas, and new experiences.

The joy of learning keeps your mind young, your attitude humble, and your skills sharp.

Competence gets you the job; **curiosity keeps you employable for life.**

Final Dose: Keep Your Learning Muscles Active

The Skill-Upgradation Vaccine is not a one-time shot — it's a **lifelong booster**.

Each time you learn, unlearn, or relearn, you strengthen your professional immunity against redundancy and irrelevance.

So, keep your curiosity alive.

Stay open. Stay relevant. Stay *Always in Beta.*

In the future of work, your degree gets you in — your learning agility keeps you in.

The Skill-Upgradation Vaccine ensures that no matter how industries evolve,

you remain *relevant, resourceful, and resilient.*

CHAPTER 8

MENTORSHIP VACCINE (VIRAL VECTOR) – ABSORB WISDOM FROM SENIORS.

This is one of the most powerful vaccines in your **Career Immunity Framework** — the **Mentorship Vaccine (Viral Vector).**

Just like a **viral vector vaccine** uses a harmless virus to deliver critical instructions that trigger protection, **mentorship** helps new professionals receive *wisdom, shortcuts, and survival codes* from those who've already walked the path — safely and effectively.

Because the fastest way to learn is through someone else's experience.

Just as viral vector vaccines safely deliver protective genetic information, mentors deliver **decoded experience** — real-world lessons, unspoken rules, and invisible pathways — that help you avoid common traps and accelerate growth.

Story: "Rahul and the Mentorship Vaccine"- *The Lessons That Fast-Tracked His Growth*

Rahul joined a reputed tech consulting firm straight out of engineering college. Bright and ambitious, he wanted to prove himself quickly — working long hours, volunteering for every project, and trying to impress his seniors with speed and independence.

However, within six months, he began to struggle. He was overworked, often redoing tasks that could have been avoided, and missing subtle expectations that weren't written anywhere. His effort was huge, but his impact was small.

One evening, his project director, Meera, called him in and said gently,

"Rahul, you're running fast, but not always in the right direction. You don't have to make every mistake yourself — that's what mentors are for."

She offered to guide him informally. Rahul began meeting her for 15 minutes every Friday. Instead of asking for solutions, he asked for *perspective*:

- "How do you prepare for stakeholder meetings?"
- "What mistakes do new consultants make?"
- "How do you prioritize when everything seems urgent?"

Meera didn't micromanage — she simply shared stories of her own early blunders and the lessons behind them.

Rahul started applying these insights immediately: preparing questions before every client call, documenting assumptions, and communicating proactively.

Within months, his work quality improved dramatically. Senior clients began trusting him. He became known for clarity and composure — rare traits for his experience level.

A year later, when Meera moved to a global role, she recommended Rahul to lead a sub-project — two years ahead of his peers.

In his farewell note to her, Rahul wrote:

"You didn't just mentor me — you vaccinated me. Your experiences protected me from the mistakes I would have made on my own."

Years later, as Rahul became a manager himself, he started mentoring new trainees every year — passing on the "immunity" that once saved him.

Prescription for Corporate New Joinees to Build the Mentorship Vaccine

Building Lifelong Immunity Through Guidance and Growth

In the corporate world, success is not a solo sport. Behind every accomplished professional stands a network of mentors — people who offered insight, direction, and encouragement when it mattered most. The **Mentorship Vaccine** is your dose of collective wisdom — a way to accelerate your learning curve, avoid preventable mistakes, and cultivate professional maturity through meaningful guidance.

Mentorship doesn't just make your journey easier; it makes it deeper. It helps you learn not just *what* to do, but *how* to think. The right mentor can save you years of trial and error, but only if you learn how to seek and sustain that relationship thoughtfully.

Here's how new joinees can build and benefit from their **Mentorship Vaccine**:

Dose 1. Seek, Don't Wait

Great mentors rarely fall into your lap — you have to *seek them out.* Look around your workplace and identify professionals who inspire you, not just through their titles but through their work ethic, attitude, and clarity of purpose.

Approach them respectfully. A simple, sincere message like, *"I really admire how you handled that project — may I occasionally seek your guidance?"* often opens doors.

Remember, mentorship is not a privilege reserved for a few; it's an opportunity created by the proactive. Most experienced professionals are more than willing to guide those who show genuine curiosity and commitment.

Dose 2. Be Curious, Not Clingy

A strong mentorship thrives on respect and preparation. When you get time with a mentor, come with specific questions, challenges, or reflections — not casual chatter.

Good mentees show they value their mentor's time by being focused, concise, and curious.

You don't need to be in touch daily; meaningful conversations, even if infrequent, can be transformative when you're truly engaged.

Dose 3. Learn from Many Mentors

Don't look for one perfect mentor to solve every problem. Your growth is multi-dimensional — and so should your mentorship be.

One mentor may guide your **technical expertise**, another your **communication style**, and another your **strategic thinking**.

By learning from multiple mentors, you build a balanced and resilient professional identity. This diversity of wisdom creates a broader immunity — protecting you from narrow perspectives and reinforcing your adaptability.

Dose 4. Listen for Context, Not Commands

Mentors share experiences, not instructions. Their advice worked in a certain context — a specific time, culture, or organization.

Don't follow suggestions blindly; instead, seek to understand *why* something worked for them and *how* it can be adapted to your situation.

True mentorship is not imitation — it's interpretation. The goal is to extract principles, not replicate playbooks.

Dose 5. Show Progress

Mentors feel most fulfilled when they see their guidance in action. Always share how their advice helped you — whether it improved your performance, changed your approach, or solved a problem.

This not only motivates them but also deepens the bond of trust. It turns your relationship from transactional to transformational.

Dose 6. Be Mentorable

The first rule of being mentored is being *coachable.* Accept feedback without defensiveness.

Mentorship fails not because of poor advice, but because of resistance to growth.

Approach every piece of feedback as a gift — even if it's uncomfortable. Ego blocks evolution; humility accelerates it.

Dose 7. Document Mentor Wisdom

Start maintaining a **Mentorship Journal** — a personal notebook or digital log where you capture the essence of your mentor's insights: quotes, key lessons, questions that made you think, and mental models they shared.

Over time, this becomes your **Career Immunity Manual** — a living document of your evolution, built from the distilled wisdom of those who walked the path before you.

Dose 8. Pay It Forward

The cycle of mentorship is incomplete until you pass it on. As you grow in experience, offer guidance to juniors, interns, or new team members.

Teaching reinforces your own learning and strengthens the organization's collective intelligence.

Remember, true career immunity is **collective, not individual.** A healthy corporate ecosystem is one where everyone is learning, guiding, and growing together.

Final Dose: Mentorship is a Two-Way Vaccine

Mentorship not only strengthens you but also energizes your mentors — it's a mutual exchange of curiosity and wisdom. As a new joinee, approach mentorship not as dependency but as *co-evolution.*

Every conversation, every piece of advice, every honest feedback becomes a micro-dose of immunity — protecting you from burnout, confusion, and stagnation.

Seek wisdom. Stay humble. Pass it on. That's the true power of the Mentorship Vaccine.

A mentor is a living vaccine — they've faced the infection and built immunity.

By learning from their journey, you don't just gain advice — you inherit protection.

Seek mentors early. Absorb deeply. Share widely. That's how careers — and cultures — thrive.

CHAPTER 9

TIME-MANAGEMENT VACCINE – PROTECTS FROM BURNOUT AND MISSED DEADLINES.

Because productivity without recovery is a short-term win and a long-term loss.

The Time-Management Vaccine helps you build resistance against the two biggest corporate infections: **chaos** and **burnout**.

It's not about doing more — it's about doing what matters *at the right time, with the right energy.*

This one is vital for long-term career *stamina.*

Here's a **story** that illustrates how the "Time-Management Vaccine" protects professionals from burnout and chaos — followed by Prescription for new joiners to build this immunity.

Story: "Neha and the Time-Management Vaccine"- *From Burnout to Balance*

Neha joined a fast-growing marketing agency as a management trainee — excited, ambitious, and determined to make a mark. In her first few months, she took every task that came her way. "The more I do, the more I'll learn," she told herself.

Soon, her days began to blur.

She was replying to emails during lunch, skipping gym sessions, staying up late tweaking presentations. Her weekends became extensions of weekdays. Deadlines were met — barely — but her energy was draining fast.

One morning, Neha missed a key client call because she overslept after working till 3 a.m. The client was furious. Her manager called her in and said calmly:

"Neha, hard work is admirable, but smart work is sustainable. You don't need more hours — you need better structure."

That's when Neha decided to take her **Time-Management Vaccine**.

She began with small doses:

- Every evening, she planned her top three priorities for the next day.
- She blocked "deep work" hours in the morning — no emails, no multitasking.
- She used a simple rule: *If it takes less than 2 minutes, do it now; if not, schedule it.*

- She started saying "no" to tasks that didn't align with her goals.

Gradually, her stress reduced. She had more clarity, better control, and even time for herself. Her reports were on time, presentations sharper, and energy higher.

Three months later, the same client who once complained praised her for "professionalism and consistency."

When her manager nominated her for a fast-track promotion, he said,

"Neha didn't just manage time — she mastered attention."

By vaccinating herself with structure, Neha had achieved something more powerful than productivity — **peace with purpose**.

Prescription for Corporate New Joinees to Build the Time-Management Vaccine

Time management is the **most powerful immunity booster** in the corporate ecosystem. Without it, even the brightest professionals succumb to stress, burnout, and missed opportunities. This vaccine is a series of practical doses — each designed to help you build resilience, focus, and a rhythm that keeps you thriving in fast-paced corporate life.

Dose 1: Plan Before You Begin – The Daily Blueprint Shot

Start your day with a **10-minute planning ritual** — your personal "morning briefing."

- List your top three priorities, key meetings, and tasks that must move forward today.
- Schedule focus blocks and buffer zones before surprises hit.
- Remember, planning is not a delay — it's a **time multiplier**. Ten minutes of clarity in the morning can save hours of confusion later.

Dose 2: Apply the 3P Rule – Prioritize, Plan, Protect

This is your **core immunity booster**.

- **Prioritize:** Identify tasks that create meaningful outcomes, not just motion.
- **Plan:** Break big goals into daily or hourly milestones.
- **Protect:** Guard your high-focus hours from distractions — silence notifications, close unnecessary tabs, and make yourself "unavailable" when deep work demands it.

When you protect your priorities, you protect your peace.

Dose 3: Reject the Multitasking Myth – The Focus Serum

Multitasking seems efficient but actually **weakens your cognitive immunity**.

- Each switch between tasks drains mental energy — like constantly rebooting your brain.
- Finish one task fully, celebrate that small win, and move to the next.

Deep focus is a **career superpower** few develop early. Start now.

Dose 4: Use Tools as Allies – The Productivity Kit

Technology can either be a **booster or a barrier** — depending on how you use it.

- Use task boards like **Trello, Asana, or Notion**, or even a well-structured notebook.
- Block your calendar for thinking time, not just meetings.
- Review weekly to identify where your hours truly go — and what drains your energy.

Smart tools don't manage your time — **they help you manage yourself**.

Dose 5: Manage Energy, Not Just Hours – The Rhythm Regulator

Peak productivity is not about working longer, but working at the **right energy levels**.

- Schedule demanding tasks during your mental high zones — usually mornings for most people.
- Reserve afternoons for routine or collaborative work.
- Track your natural energy rhythm and design your day around it.

Time management without energy management is like running a marathon on low fuel.

Dose 6: Learn to Say "No" Gracefully – The Immunity Shield

Saying yes to everything weakens your defences.

- If your bandwidth is full, decline respectfully: "I'd love to contribute, but my current priorities might delay this. Can we explore next week or delegate support?"

- Protect your focus from being spread too thin.

Every "no" to distraction is a "yes" to meaningful work.

Dose 7: Batch and Buffer – The Efficiency Booster

The corporate virus of chaos thrives in random, unstructured schedules.

- **Batch similar tasks** (emails, reports, calls) to reduce switching fatigue.
- Always add a **15–20% buffer** in project timelines. Delays happen — be ready.

Predictable structure builds trust. When you deliver consistently, your credibility compounds.

Dose 8: Use Breaks as Boosters – The Focus Recharge Dose

Work without recovery causes burnout.

- Take short breaks every **75–90 minutes** — stretch, hydrate, or take a short walk.
- Avoid guilt for pausing — rest is not a reward; it's part of high performance.

Regular breaks reboot your focus and creativity — making you stronger, not slower.

Dose 9: Track, Reflect, Improve – The Continuous Immunization Cycle

Time mastery is a lifelong vaccine that needs **regular boosters**.

- Every week, review how you spent your hours: What gave value? What drained it?
- Eliminate, automate, or delegate low-impact activities.

Reflection turns experience into expertise.

Dose 10: Set Work–Life Boundaries Early – The Sustainability Dose

True productivity includes **personal recovery**.

- Disconnect from emails and work messages after hours whenever possible.
- Guard your weekends and family time as sacred.
- Sleep well, move daily, and nurture hobbies — they are your **long-term immunity builders**.

When you manage time wisely, life rewards you with both success and serenity.

Final Dose: Time is not money — it's **life energy**. The Time-Management Vaccine helps you invest that energy consciously so that every hour moves you closer to excellence, not exhaustion.

Time management is not about controlling the clock — it's about directing your attention.

When you master your focus, you protect your energy, reputation, and mental health.

That's true career immunity — *the ability to sustain excellence without exhaustion.*

CHAPTER 10

RESILIENCE VACCINE – BUILDS STAMINA FOR SETBACKS AND FAILURES.

Because in the corporate world, the only constant is change — and challenges are inevitable.

This vaccine strengthens your **mental stamina, adaptability, and learning from failure**, so you can face setbacks without losing direction, confidence, or motivation.

The **Resilience Vaccine** is the ultimate booster for *career longevity.*

It protects professionals from the inevitable setbacks, failures, and rejections in the corporate world, ensuring they don't just survive — they thrive.

Here's a **story** first, followed by **Prescription** for building this vaccine.

Story: "Siddharth and the Resilience Vaccine"- *Bouncing Back Stronger*

Siddharth joined a leading FMCG company as a sales associate. Energetic and ambitious, he quickly took on challenging clients and high-value accounts. Within six months, he faced his first major setback — a major client he had nurtured for months suddenly switched to a competitor due to pricing issues.

Siddharth was devastated. He felt responsible and questioned his abilities. His confidence dipped, and he started avoiding challenging accounts, thinking he'd fail again.

One day, his mentor noticed his reluctance and said:

"Siddharth, failure is not the opposite of success — it's part of it. Every setback is a rehearsal for your next win."

Inspired, Siddharth decided to "take his Resilience Vaccine."

He began small:

- Analyzing what went wrong without blaming himself or others.
- Seeking feedback from seniors and peers.
- Rewriting his client approach strategy based on lessons learned.

Gradually, he started pitching again, experimenting with new strategies, and accepting rejections as data points rather than disasters.

Six months later, he closed a client account even bigger than the one he had lost. The leadership team praised his persistence, and he became a role model for handling setbacks with composure.

Years later, Siddharth shared his philosophy with new joiners:

"Resilience isn't about never failing — it's about failing forward, learning fast, and refusing to stay down. That's the strongest immunity a career can have."

Prescription for Corporate New Joinees to Build the Resilience Vaccine

Resilience is your **corporate immune system** — the inner strength that helps you recover from setbacks, adapt to change, and keep growing despite pressure.

Every challenge you face in the workplace — a failed project, harsh feedback, missed promotion, or unexpected change — is not a threat, but a chance to strengthen your immunity.

These ten doses of the **Resilience Vaccine** will prepare you to bounce back stronger every time life tests your professional stamina.

Dose 1: Normalize Failure Early – The Acceptance Injection

The first step toward resilience is to **accept failure as part of growth**, not the end of it.

- Mistakes are **inevitable learning signals**, not career-defining disasters.
- Every successful leader has a trail of failures behind them — the difference is how they responded.

Instead of asking *"Why me?"*, ask *"What is this teaching me?"*

The sooner you normalize failure, the faster you build emotional immunity.

Dose 2: Analyze, Don't Internalize – The Reflection Serum

When something goes wrong, separate **the event** from **your identity**.

- Break down the failure objectively: Was it a process flaw? Communication gap? Unrealistic timeline?
- Avoid emotional over-attachment to outcomes. Self-blame weakens clarity.

Reflection turns pain into progress.

Remember: **Analysis strengthens you; internalization drains you.**

Dose 3: Develop a Growth Mindset – The Mind Muscle Booster

A resilient professional doesn't fear challenges; they **see them as training grounds**.

- Replace "I failed" with "I learned."
- After every tough phase, ask: "How can I grow from this?"

Each experience — good or bad — becomes a micro-dose of **career evolution**.

Growth mindset converts every obstacle into an opportunity for renewal.

Dose 4: Build Emotional Regulation Skills – The Stability Pill

Resilience is not just endurance — it's **emotional balance under pressure**.

- Practice mindfulness, deep breathing, or journaling to calm your internal storm.
- Reflect daily on what triggered stress and how you responded.

Emotional regulation doesn't remove stress — **it teaches you to dance with it gracefully.**

Calm minds make confident decisions.

Dose 5: Seek Support – The Connection Booster

No one builds resilience in isolation.

- Reach out to mentors, peers, or managers when facing tough moments.
- Sometimes, an outside perspective can reveal solutions hidden by your stress.
- Sharing your struggles creates psychological safety — for you and for others.

Remember: **asking for help is not weakness; it's wisdom.**

Dose 6: Start Small to Rebuild Confidence – The Recovery Shot

After a setback, don't rush to prove yourself. Start with **small, achievable wins**.

- Complete one manageable project, meet one realistic goal, or fix one broken process.

- Each micro-success restores momentum and rebuilds your self-trust.

Confidence is not rebuilt overnight — it grows dose by dose through consistent action.

Dose 7: Prepare a Contingency Mindset – The Preventive Dose

Resilience is not just reacting to problems — it's **anticipating them**.

- Before every project or decision, ask: "What if this doesn't go as planned?"
- Prepare alternate routes and responses in advance.

When you mentally rehearse setbacks, real ones feel less intimidating.

A prepared mind rarely panics — it pivots.

Dose 8: Maintain Perspective – The Vision Stabilizer

Resilient professionals keep their **eyes on the horizon**, not the pothole.

- One failure does not define your career; it's a single scene, not the entire story.
- Zoom out — focus on the big picture and long-term trajectory.
- Remember that setbacks often redirect you to something better aligned with your growth.

Perspective transforms pain into purpose.

Dose 9: Document Lessons Learned – The Learning Log Vaccine

Keep a **"Resilience Journal"** — your private record of growth through adversity.

- Write what went wrong, what you discovered, and how you adapted.
- Over time, this journal becomes your **career survival manual** — a library of your hard-earned wisdom.

Reflection cements learning and helps you respond smarter the next time life tests you.

Dose 10: Help Others Bounce Back – The Immunity Multiplier

True resilience becomes powerful when it's **shared**.

- Support a colleague going through a rough patch; share your recovery stories and lessons.
- When you help others rise, you reinforce your own strength and leadership maturity.
- A resilient team is far stronger than a resilient individual.

Resilience multiplies when it moves from *"me"* to *"we."*

Final Dose: Resilience doesn't mean you never fall — it means you **never stop rising.**

Each challenge you face is a controlled dose that strengthens your emotional, mental, and professional immunity.

The stronger your resilience, the more fearless your career journey becomes.

CHAPTER 11

CONFLICT-RESOLUTION VACCINE – PREVENTS ESCALATION OF WORKPLACE DISPUTES.

Because every unresolved conflict is a hidden career risk.

This vaccine equips new professionals with **tools to manage tension, mediate effectively, and maintain relationships**, ensuring disputes don't derail performance or reputation.

The **Conflict-Resolution Vaccine** is essential for career immunity, because workplace disputes are inevitable, but escalation is optional.

Here's a **story** first to illustrate how an employee uses this vaccine to thrive, followed by **Prescription** for new joiners.

Story: "Kavita and the Conflict-Resolution Vaccine"- *Turning Tension into Trust*

Kavita joined a mid-sized IT firm as a project coordinator. She was diligent, proactive, and loved solving problems. However, early in her role, she noticed friction between two senior team members — one in development, one in design. Their disagreements over timelines and responsibilities were starting to delay project milestones.

At first, Kavita avoided getting involved. But one day, a heated argument disrupted a client call. The project manager asked her to step in and mediate.

Kavita realized this was her "Conflict-Resolution Vaccine" moment. She didn't try to take sides; instead, she applied three simple principles:

1. **Listen Actively:** She gave each party uninterrupted time to explain their concerns.
2. **Seek Common Ground:** She highlighted shared goals — delivering the project on time and with quality.
3. **Propose Collaborative Solutions:** She suggested a clear division of responsibilities and regular check-ins.

The tension eased immediately. Over the next few weeks, Kavita continued to monitor communication and facilitated small clarifications proactively. The project completed successfully and on time.

Her manager later praised her:

"Kavita doesn't just manage tasks — she manages relationships. That's rare in someone this junior."

Years later, Kavita was promoted to team lead. She often says:

"Conflict is inevitable. Escalation is optional. Learning to resolve disputes before they explode is like career insurance."

Prescription for Corporate New Joinees to Build the Conflict-Resolution Vaccine

In every organization, conflict is inevitable — but chaos is optional. Workplace disagreements, differing opinions, or clashing priorities are natural byproducts of ambition and diversity. What distinguishes professionals who thrive is not the absence of conflict, but the *presence of composure and clarity* in navigating it.

This **Conflict-Resolution Vaccine** helps new joinees build emotional antibodies against misunderstandings, miscommunication, and ego-driven clashes. Each dose strengthens your ability to respond with maturity, empathy, and professionalism — creating harmony without compromising results.

Dose 1: Stay Calm and Neutral

Before responding to any heated situation, pause. Take a breath.

Your calm is your credibility. When emotions rise, the one who stays grounded earns trust automatically. Avoid rushing to conclusions or choosing sides without complete facts. Neutrality allows you to become the *bridge*, not the barrier.

Remember — the loudest voice rarely wins; the calmest mind usually does.

Dose 2: Listen First, Speak Later

Most conflicts persist because people listen to reply, not to understand.

When a disagreement surfaces, let others express their viewpoints fully. Ask questions to clarify, not to corner. Reflect what you hear — "So you're saying the deadline felt unrealistic?" — this builds empathy and trust.

True listening diffuses tension faster than argument ever can.

Dose 3: Focus on Interests, Not Positions

People often defend their *positions* ("I'm right"), but what they truly care about are *interests* ("I want this project to succeed"). Shift the discussion from *who's right* to *what's right.*

Highlight shared goals such as customer satisfaction, team success, or quality delivery. When people see the larger mission, personal clashes shrink in size and importance.

Dose 4: Communicate Clearly and Professionally

Language can heal or harm — choose your words wisely.

Use calm, factual, and respectful statements:

- Replace "You're wrong" with "I see it differently."
- Avoid sarcasm or emotional exaggerations.
- Focus on outcomes, not accusations.

The tone you use becomes the temperature of the room — keep it cool and constructive.

Dose 5: Seek Solutions, Not Victory

A mature professional doesn't aim to "win" a conflict — they aim to *resolve* it.

Think in terms of "What's best for the team or the project?" rather than "Who's right?"

Propose practical compromises, set up structured discussions, or suggest preventive measures. Resolution is progress; victory is vanity.

Dose 6: Document Key Agreements

After discussions, capture conclusions and next steps in writing.

A simple follow-up email like *"Just summarizing our discussion — here's what we agreed..."* prevents confusion later.

Documentation protects professionalism and ensures accountability without confrontation. It's a subtle shield that saves future stress.

Dose 7: Escalate Only When Necessary

Conflicts don't always need referees. Try to resolve issues directly with involved parties first. Escalate to a manager or HR only when all reasonable attempts fail or when conflict disrupts productivity.

Escalation is a last resort, not a shortcut to avoid difficult conversations.

Dose 8: Build Empathy and Rapport

Most conflicts are symptoms of misunderstanding.

Take time to know your colleagues — their workloads, priorities, and pressures. When you understand *why* someone reacts a certain way, you stop taking things personally. Empathy converts potential friction into collaboration.

Dose 9: Reflect and Learn

After resolving any conflict, reflect privately:

- What triggered it?
- What did I handle well?
- What could I do differently next time?

Each reflection boosts your emotional intelligence — your immunity to future disputes.

Dose 10: Model Conflict-Resolution Behavior

Your behavior becomes the culture others imitate.

When you handle disagreements with grace, transparency, and logic, others follow suit. You become the *peace anchor* — the professional who can be trusted in turbulent times. That reputation is one of the strongest forms of career capital.

Final Booster Dose:

Conflict isn't the opposite of collaboration — it's a test of it.

Those who master the art of resolving tension without losing trust don't just survive in corporate life — they *lead it.*

Conflict is inevitable; escalation is optional.

The Conflict-Resolution Vaccine ensures that disagreements strengthen collaboration instead of eroding trust.

By staying composed, listening actively, and seeking solutions, you protect both relationships and career trajectory.

CHAPTER 12

FINANCIAL-LITERACY VACCINE – IMMUNIZES AGAINST MONEY MISMANAGEMENT (SALARY, TAXES, SAVINGS).

Because financial stress is one of the biggest hidden career threats.

This vaccine strengthens your **ability to manage salary, taxes, savings, and investments**, allowing you to stay focused, independent, and stress-free in your professional journey.

The **Financial-Literacy Vaccine** is a critical part of long-term career immunity. It protects employees from stress, poor financial decisions, and dependency, ensuring they can focus fully on growth and opportunities.

Here's a **story** first, followed by **Prescription** for new joiners.

Story: "Rohit and the Financial-Literacy Vaccine"- *From Paycheck Panic to Financial Confidence*

Rohit joined a mid-sized IT firm as a software engineer. Excited about his first corporate salary, he started spending freely — new gadgets, dining out, and weekend trips. At the same time, he ignored deductions, taxes, and long-term savings.

Within six months, an unexpected expense — a medical emergency in his family — wiped out his savings. Stress mounted, and he realized that while he was growing professionally, he had neglected financial resilience.

Determined to regain control, Rohit decided to take his **Financial-Literacy Vaccine**.

He began with three steps:

1. **Budgeting:** He tracked income, fixed expenses, and set aside a fixed portion for savings.
2. **Tax Awareness:** He understood salary components, tax-saving options, and deductions.
3. **Investments & Emergency Fund:** He opened a recurring deposit and a SIP, creating a safety net for unforeseen circumstances.

Soon, Rohit noticed that money stress no longer distracted him from work. He could focus on delivering projects and learning new skills. Within two years, he was debt-free, had an emergency fund covering six months of expenses, and even started investing for long-term goals like a home and retirement.

At a company town hall, he shared his journey with juniors:

"Financial literacy isn't just about money — it's about freedom and focus. Once your money works for you, your career can too."

Rohit's discipline and clarity also caught the attention of management, leading to a promotion and a leadership training opportunity. His professional and financial growth had become intertwined.

Prescription for Corporate New Joinees to Build the Financial-Literacy Vaccine

Money is more than a paycheck — it's your career's silent partner.

For most corporate professionals, the early years are filled with enthusiasm for learning, performance, and promotions. Yet, very few focus on learning the one skill that ensures peace of mind and long-term security — *financial literacy.*

A financially aware employee performs better because they are not distracted by financial anxiety. This **Financial-Literacy Vaccine** helps new joinees build immunity against poor financial decisions, impulsive spending, and long-term money stress.

Each dose strengthens your ability to plan, protect, and prosper — ensuring your career rewards translate into sustainable wealth.

Dose 1: Track Every Rupee — Awareness Is Immunity

The first step to financial health is awareness.

Keep a simple record of your monthly cash flow — how much comes in, how much goes out, and where it goes. Categorize your spending into *essentials*, *comforts*, and *extras*.

Tracking money daily (even briefly) builds mindfulness and curbs wasteful habits. When you know your numbers, you control them — not the other way around.

Dose 2: Decode Your Salary Slip — Know What You Earn

Many new employees only look at the *take-home* figure, ignoring the structure behind it.

Understand the difference between **CTC (Cost to Company), gross pay**, and **net pay**. Learn what components — like HRA, PF, ESIC, bonuses, and gratuity — actually mean.

When you know what's taxable, what's reimbursable, and what's a benefit, you can plan smarter and avoid end-of-year tax shocks.

Dose 3: Build an Emergency Fund — Your Financial Vaccine Booster

Life is unpredictable — layoffs, medical bills, or unexpected family needs can arise anytime.

Set aside **3–6 months of living expenses** in a liquid savings or short-term fund. This buffer gives you breathing room to make calm decisions during crises.

Without this cushion, even small setbacks can feel like earthquakes. An emergency fund is your corporate shock absorber.

Dose 4: Start Investing Early — Let Time Work for You

The best time to invest was yesterday. The second-best time is now.

Start small — even a modest monthly **Systematic Investment Plan (SIP)** in a mutual fund can grow into a substantial corpus over time.

Understand the power of compounding: money grows exponentially when you give it time and consistency. Early starters gain the most — because compounding rewards patience, not income level.

Dose 5: Learn Tax Planning — Keep More of What You Earn

Taxes are not punishments; they're systems that can be optimized with knowledge.

Learn about **Section 80C deductions, HRA exemptions, NPS benefits,** and **health insurance deductions**.

Plan your investments with tax-saving instruments like ELSS, PPF, or insurance-linked savings plans. A little planning today saves both money and stress later.

Dose 6: Resist Lifestyle Inflation — Upgrade Mindset, Not Just Possessions

The moment your salary rises, your expenses will try to follow.

Avoid falling into the "upgrade trap" — new phone, new car, expensive dining — all justified as "I deserve it."

Increase spending only after you've increased savings proportionally. Let your **financial goals**, not peer pressure, decide your lifestyle.

Dose 7: Use Financial Tools and Apps — Technology as Your Treasurer

Your smartphone can be your accountant.

Use apps like **Walnut, Money Manager, Mint, or Goodbudget** to track expenses automatically.

Set reminders for bill payments, credit card dues, and SIPs.

Automation is the modern vitamin for financial discipline — it ensures consistency without daily effort.

Dose 8: Keep Learning — Financial Literacy Is a Lifelong Course

Money management isn't a one-time topic; it's a lifelong curriculum.

Read books like *"Rich Dad, Poor Dad"* or *"The Psychology of Money."* Attend online financial literacy webinars. Follow credible finance educators or advisors.

Each new concept you learn — from mutual funds to insurance — adds another antibody against ignorance.

💊 Dose 9: Separate Short-Term and Long-Term Goals — Clarity Is Key

Not all financial goals are created equal.

- **Short-term goals:** Emergency fund, debt repayment, short travel plans.
- **Long-term goals:** Buying a house, children's education, retirement corpus.

Create different savings or investment channels for each. When your money has a clear purpose, it grows with discipline.

💊 Dose 10: Review Regularly — Immunity Requires Boosters

Your financial plan should evolve with your career.

Review your income, investments, and expenses every **quarter**. Adjust your strategy as your salary, dependents, or priorities change.

Financial stability is not about perfection — it's about consistent awareness and timely recalibration.

Final Booster Dose

Wealth creation isn't about how much you earn — it's about how wisely you manage, grow, and protect what you have.

Financial literacy transforms money from a source of stress into a source of strength.

For the modern professional, *financial health is career health.*

Financial literacy is a career booster, not just a life skill.

Money stress drains focus, creativity, and confidence. By taking the Financial-Literacy Vaccine early, you protect your mental bandwidth and unlock freedom to excel professionally.

Career Vaccines: Growth, Visibility, and Strategic Edge

Once you have built your core immunity with the first 10 vaccines, the next set prepares you to thrive, stand out, and expand influence. These vaccines equip you to think strategically, innovate, communicate effectively, and position yourself for accelerated career growth.

B. Growth Vaccines (Immunity – Middle Level)

CHAPTER 13

ADAPTABILITY VACCINE (TRAVEL) – HANDLE TRANSFERS, MERGERS, GLOBAL CULTURES.

Because the only constant in the corporate world is change.

This vaccine strengthens your **ability to adjust quickly, embrace new roles, and work effectively across teams and cultures**, turning potential disruptions into opportunities.

The **Adaptability Vaccine (Travel)** is crucial for corporate immunity in today's dynamic workplaces.

It equips employees to **thrive through transfers, mergers, shifting roles, and diverse global cultures.**

Here's a **story** first, followed by **practical prescription** for corporate employees.

Story: "Isha and the Adaptability Vaccine"- *Thriving Amid Change*

Isha joined a multinational FMCG company as a marketing analyst. She was comfortable in her initial role and her regional team, excelling at local campaigns.

Six months in, the company underwent a merger. Her team was restructured, new reporting lines were introduced, and she was asked to temporarily support a team in a different country. Isha felt anxious — different time zones, unfamiliar workflows, and a new cultural context were intimidating.

Instead of resisting, she treated it as her **Adaptability Vaccine** moment.

Steps she took:

1. **Observing & Learning:** She spent the first week understanding new processes, cultural norms, and team dynamics.
2. **Asking Questions:** She sought guidance from local colleagues, respecting their practices while sharing her own insights.
3. **Flexibility in Communication:** Adjusted her communication style to suit global colleagues — concise emails for some, collaborative video calls for others.
4. **Embracing Change Mindset:** She reframed the situation as an opportunity to gain cross-cultural experience and new skills.

Over the next few months, Isha became a bridge between regional and global teams, improving workflow efficiency and building strong international relationships. Her adaptability impressed leadership, and she was later offered a permanent rotational role that accelerated her career growth.

Isha's reflection:

"Change is inevitable. Adaptability is your career seatbelt — it keeps you steady, even when the corporate ride gets bumpy."

Prescription for Corporate Employees to Build the Adaptability Vaccine

In today's rapidly changing corporate world, adaptability is not just a skill — it's a survival vaccine. The ability to pivot, learn, and thrive amidst constant transformation ensures that you remain relevant, confident, and resilient throughout your career. Below are the **10 Adaptability Doses** every professional must take regularly for full corporate immunity.

Dose 1: Embrace Change as a Learning Opportunity

Change is the only constant in any organization. Instead of resisting it, view every disruption — be it a new manager, merger, or system — as a classroom for growth.

- **Shift perspective:** Ask, "What can I learn here?" instead of "Why is this happening to me?"
- **Adopt curiosity:** Explore how new changes align with your long-term professional goals.
- **Remember:** Every evolution brings hidden opportunities for advancement.

Dose 2: Observe and Understand Before Acting

When entering new teams or environments, resist the urge to make immediate changes. Adaptability begins with awareness.

- **Take time to observe** workflows, personalities, and unwritten team norms.
- **Ask clarifying questions** to understand "why things work this way."
- **Once you adapt, contribute:** Thoughtful suggestions are valued when grounded in context.

Dose 3: Be Open to New Roles and Challenges

Growth doesn't come from comfort. Taking on new responsibilities builds your "flexibility muscles."

- **Volunteer** for projects outside your expertise.
- **Say yes** to rotational roles, task forces, or short-term assignments.
- **Outcome:** You'll gain multidimensional experience and position yourself as a go-to problem solver.

Dose 4: Develop Cultural Awareness

Global teams bring diverse work styles and expectations. Cultural intelligence is a superpower for modern professionals.

- **Learn and respect** local customs, holidays, and communication preferences.
- **Avoid assumptions:** Observe how your colleagues express disagreement or feedback.

- **Small gestures matter:** A culturally aware attitude builds bridges and mutual respect.

Dose 5: Communicate Effectively Across Geographies

Strong communication sustains adaptability. It ensures you stay aligned even when teams are spread across time zones.

- **Adapt your communication mode:** Some prefer detailed emails; others, short chats or calls.
- **Be mindful of tone and timing:** Respect global work hours and avoid overloading inboxes.
- **Result:** Clear, respectful communication prevents misunderstandings and strengthens teamwork.

Dose 6: Stay Calm Amid Ambiguity

Adaptable professionals remain steady when directions are unclear or priorities shift.

- **Pause and breathe** before reacting.
- **Clarify expectations:** Politely ask for priorities and next steps.
- **Stay solution-oriented:** Focus on what can be done rather than what's uncertain.
- **Remember:** Calmness during chaos earns trust and leadership credibility.

Dose 7: Document and Share Best Practices

Change brings learning — and sharing that learning multiplies its value.

- **Keep notes** of processes, shortcuts, and lessons from transitions.

- **Create guides or SOPs** that help others adapt faster.
- **Outcome:** You become a knowledge hub, fostering a culture of collaboration and preparedness.

Dose 8: Build a Global Network

Connections beyond your immediate circle enhance adaptability. They offer insights, ideas, and support during change.

- **Engage** with peers across departments, geographies, or industries.
- **Participate** in cross-functional meetings and global initiatives.
- **Result:** When change hits, your network becomes your safety net and opportunity pool.

Dose 9: Be Resilient with Feedback

Feedback is not rejection; it's direction. Adaptable employees use it as raw material for growth.

- **Listen actively** without defensiveness.
- **Reflect and apply** actionable parts immediately.
- **Remember:** The faster you respond to feedback, the faster you evolve.

Dose 10: Celebrate Small Wins Along the Way

Adaptability is a journey, not a one-time act. Recognizing your progress keeps you motivated.

- **Acknowledge** every time you successfully adjust to a new situation.
- **Reward yourself** — even small milestones matter.

- **Outcome:** Confidence compounds, and each win strengthens your immunity to future change.

Final Dose:

Adaptability isn't about being perfect in every situation — it's about staying open, grounded, and proactive. The more doses you take, the stronger your corporate immunity becomes. When change strikes next, you won't just survive — you'll thrive.

Adaptability is the ultimate career armor.

Transfers, mergers, and global shifts are not threats — they're opportunities for accelerated growth.

The more flexible and culturally aware you are, the stronger your career immunity becomes.

CHAPTER 14

FEEDBACK VACCINE – CONVERT CRITICISM INTO GROWTH FUEL.

Because constructive criticism is one of the fastest ways to upgrade your skills and reputation.

This vaccine strengthens your **ability to receive, process, and act on feedback** effectively, ensuring you improve continuously rather than reacting emotionally.

The **Feedback Vaccine** is one of the most transformative in the Career Immunity framework.

It helps employees **use criticism, appraisals, and suggestions as fuel for growth**, rather than letting feedback demoralize or derail them.

Here's a **story** first, followed by **Prescription**.

Story: "Arjun and the Feedback Vaccine"-*Turning Criticism into Career Momentum*

Arjun joined a large consulting firm as a junior analyst. In his first client presentation, he had prepared extensively, but during the meeting, his manager critiqued his slides, pointed out missing data, and highlighted gaps in his analysis. Arjun felt embarrassed and defensive.

Instead of sulking or avoiding future presentations, he decided to take this as his **Feedback Vaccine moment.**

Steps he took:

1. **Listen Without Defensiveness:** He noted every point his manager made without interrupting or arguing.
2. **Ask Clarifying Questions:** He sought specific examples of what could have been improved and best practices for future work.
3. **Action Plan:** He revised the slides, cross-checked data, and incorporated storytelling techniques suggested by his manager.
4. **Follow-Up:** He presented an improved version in a smaller internal meeting, seeking additional inputs proactively.

Within a few months, Arjun became known for polished, insightful presentations. His willingness to absorb criticism, act on it, and seek continuous improvement led to recognition from senior leadership and accelerated project responsibilities.

Reflecting on his journey, Arjun said:

"Feedback is not a judgment — it's a map. Every critique is a signpost guiding you to the next level."

Prescription for Corporate Employees to Build the Feedback Vaccine

In the corporate world, **feedback is the most powerful diagnostic tool** for professional growth. Yet, many employees treat it like an uncomfortable injection — something to be avoided. The truth is, feedback, when embraced and acted upon, becomes a **career-strengthening vaccine** — one that builds resilience, clarity, and consistent improvement. Below are your **10 Doses** to build lifelong immunity to criticism and convert feedback into fuel for excellence.

Dose 1: Listen First, React Later

The first step to building your feedback immunity is to **listen with intent, not instinct**. When receiving feedback, resist the urge to interrupt, explain, or defend.

- **Treat feedback as data, not drama.** It's information about your performance, not your personality.
- **Pause and absorb.** A calm response creates space for understanding.
- **Take notes** if possible — it shows maturity and seriousness.

Remember: Reflection always works better than reaction.

Dose 2: Separate Ego from Execution

Feedback often hurts because we confuse **critique of our work** with **critique of our worth**.

- **Detach emotionally.** Remind yourself: "They are evaluating my output, not my identity."
- **Shift focus to improvement:** Ask, "What can I do better next time?" instead of "Why don't they like my work?"
- **Growth mindset:** Every piece of feedback is a stepping stone to mastery.

A strong professional ego should protect your confidence, not block your learning.

Dose 3: Clarify and Understand

Not all feedback is clear — sometimes it's vague or generic. Seek clarity before acting.

- **Ask specific questions:** "Can you give an example?" or "What would improvement look like to you?"
- **Restate key points:** "So, you're saying I should provide more detail in my reports, right?"
- **Avoid assumptions.** Misinterpreting feedback can lead to misplaced effort.

Understanding precedes transformation.

Dose 4: Prioritize Actionable Points

Trying to fix everything at once can dilute your focus. The vaccine works best when taken in small doses.

- **Identify top 2–3 action areas.** These are the most impactful or recurring ones.
- **Create a plan:** What will you start, stop, and continue doing?
- **Set short-term goals** to track visible progress.

Consistency in small improvements creates long-term transformation.

Dose 5: Implement and Iterate

Feedback without follow-up is wasted medicine. The real value lies in how quickly and effectively you act on it.

- **Apply suggestions immediately** — even small changes show responsiveness.
- **Seek micro check-ins**: "Does this new approach align better with expectations?"
- **Track your progress.** Acknowledge visible differences in performance.

Implementation converts feedback into measurable growth.

Dose 6: Seek Feedback Proactively

Don't wait for performance appraisals — build continuous feedback loops.

- **Ask for feedback regularly** from peers, managers, and mentors.
- **Frame questions positively:** "What's one thing I could do better next week?"
- **Show curiosity:** It signals self-awareness and ambition.

Proactive feedback seekers evolve faster and earn higher trust.

Dose 7: Document Your Learning

A feedback vaccine works best when tracked like a medical record.

- **Maintain a "Feedback Journal."** Record comments, insights, and your response plan.
- **Review regularly** to notice patterns and progress.
- **Over time,** this becomes your personalized "Career Development Blueprint."

Documentation turns momentary lessons into permanent wisdom.

Dose 8: Maintain Positivity

Feedback isn't a personal rejection — it's an investment in your potential.

- **Stay upbeat.** Remind yourself that only those with potential get detailed feedback.
- **Celebrate every improvement,** even minor ones.
- **Reframe criticism:** Instead of "They're being harsh," think "They care about my progress."

Positivity turns feedback into motivation, not discouragement.

Dose 9: Recognize Patterns

Repeated feedback isn't a coincidence — it's a signal.

- **Look for themes:** If multiple people highlight the same gap, it's your next growth area.
- **Address recurring issues** early — it prevents stagnation and boosts credibility.

- **Notice improvements too:** Track which areas no longer appear in reviews.

Pattern recognition transforms feedback from random input into strategic insight.

Dose 10: Thank the Giver

Feedback is an act of courage and care — few people take the time to share it.

- **Express genuine gratitude:** "Thank you for your honesty — this helps me grow."
- **Follow up later** to show progress: "Your suggestion really improved my workflow."
- **Outcome:** You'll earn trust and encourage a healthy feedback culture around you.

Gratitude sustains the cycle of mentorship and learning.

Final Dose:

Feedback is not a one-time injection; it's a recurring booster for professional growth. Each dose strengthens your confidence, deepens your awareness, and enhances your effectiveness. When you stop fearing feedback and start leveraging it, **you move from being a performer to a true professional.**

Feedback is your career's immune booster.

The stronger your Feedback Vaccine, the faster you recover from mistakes and evolve.

Professionals who embrace criticism gracefully thrive faster and gain trust, visibility, and influence.

CHAPTER 15

COMMUNICATION VACCINE – PROTECTS FROM MISUNDERSTANDINGS, BOOSTS INFLUENCE.

Because even the best work fails to create impact without clear, persuasive communication.

This vaccine strengthens your **ability to convey ideas clearly, influence outcomes, and build trust**, reducing errors, friction, and missed opportunities.

The **Communication Vaccine** is essential for career immunity because **clarity, persuasion, and relationship-building** determine long-term success in any corporate environment.

Here's a **story** first, followed by **Prescription** for new joiners and employees.

Story: "Meera and the Communication Vaccine"- *From Misunderstandings to Influence*

Meera joined a global logistics company as a project coordinator. She was highly competent but often assumed that her colleagues and clients "knew what she meant."

During one critical client call, her vague explanations caused confusion. The client escalated concerns, and internally, her manager noted that while her work was excellent, **her influence and credibility were limited due to unclear communication.**

Instead of becoming defensive, Meera decided to take her **Communication Vaccine**:

1. **Clarity First:** She started preparing concise, structured updates before every call.
2. **Active Listening:** She ensured she fully understood client and team perspectives before responding.
3. **Tailor the Message:** She adjusted her language and tone depending on audience — technical for engineers, outcome-focused for management.
4. **Feedback Loops:** She asked colleagues to confirm that her points were understood.

Within months, the impact was visible. Meetings ran smoothly, projects were executed efficiently, and stakeholders began seeking her input. Her ability to communicate effectively also led to her being invited to lead cross-departmental presentations, boosting her visibility and influence.

Meera reflected:

"Communication isn't just about speaking; it's about being understood, trusted, and remembered. That's the immunity every professional needs."

Prescription for Corporate Employees to Build the Communication Vaccine

In the corporate ecosystem, communication is the **lifeblood that carries ideas, influence, and impact**. Yet, many careers stall not because of lack of knowledge, but because of **miscommunication, unclear expression, or poor listening**. The **Communication Vaccine** builds immunity against these career viruses — confusion, misinterpretation, and misunderstanding — by strengthening your ability to convey clarity, confidence, and connection.

Below are your **10 Doses** to build communication mastery and thrive in every professional environment.

Dose 1: Be Clear and Concise

Clarity is your first line of defense in professional communication.

- **Start with the core message.** State the "what" and "why" upfront before diving into details.
- **Avoid jargon** unless everyone in the conversation understands it. Simplicity signals strength, not weakness.
- **Use structure:** Explain situations in a logical flow — *Situation → Action → Result* — to keep your listener oriented.

Remember: If people have to guess what you mean, your message has already failed.

Dose 2: Listen Actively

Great communicators are great listeners first.

- **Pay full attention** — no multitasking, no premature responses.
- **Paraphrase or summarize** what the other person says to ensure clarity and show respect.
- **Observe emotions, not just words.** Tone, pace, and pauses reveal hidden concerns.

Listening deeply prevents misdiagnosis — of people, problems, and priorities.

Dose 3: Tailor Your Message

A one-size-fits-all approach doesn't work in communication.

- **Know your audience:** A senior leader needs crisp data and outcomes, while a peer might prefer collaboration and detail.
- **Adjust tone and vocabulary:** Formal for clients, conversational for teams, inspiring for presentations.
- **Empathize with perspective:** Ask, "What does this person need to know to act?"

Effective communication is not about what you say — it's about what they understand.

Dose 4: Master Non-Verbal Communication

Your body speaks even when your mouth doesn't.

- **Maintain natural eye contact** — it signals confidence and engagement.

- **Align body language** with your message: open posture, steady gestures, and an approachable demeanor.
- **Mind your tone:** Volume, pace, and modulation can make or break your message.

Non-verbal cues are your silent ambassadors — they often communicate louder than words.

Dose 5: Ask for Feedback

Communication is a two-way vaccine — it works only when you test its effect.

- **Ask clarifying questions:** "Was that clear?" or "Does this align with your understanding?"
- **Observe reactions:** Confusion, hesitation, or silence may indicate your message didn't land.
- **Adapt based on responses:** Modify delivery, not just content.

Feedback is the mirror that shows how your words actually land — use it to refine your dosage.

Dose 6: Use Stories and Examples

Facts inform. Stories inspire.

- **Anchor your message** in relatable examples or real experiences.
- **Use storytelling frameworks:** context → challenge → action → outcome.
- **Humanize your message:** People remember emotions, not bullet points.

A well-told story turns complex ideas into memorable insights.

Dose 7: Strengthen Written Communication

Your writing often speaks before you do.

- **Structure emails and reports clearly:** Begin with *context*, specify the *action required*, and state the *deadline or outcome.*
- **Avoid long, dense paragraphs;** use bullets or numbering for clarity.
- **Proofread every message:** Typos and unclear phrasing can dilute credibility.

In corporate writing, precision is professionalism.

Dose 8: Practice Empathy in Every Interaction

Empathy is the emotional intelligence layer that binds communication together.

- **Think about impact before you speak.** Will this motivate, clarify, or discourage?
- **Acknowledge others' perspectives:** "I understand your concern" can diffuse tension instantly.
- **Respect communication preferences:** Some people prefer written summaries, others value verbal discussions.

Empathy ensures your communication heals more than it hurts.

Dose 9: Prepare for High-Stakes Conversations

Important conversations deserve rehearsal, not improvisation.

- **Plan key points:** Define your objective and anticipate counterpoints.

- **Practice delivery:** Record yourself or role-play with a trusted colleague.
- **Control emotions:** Confidence is contagious — nervousness is too.

Preparation is your immunity shot against anxiety and misfire.

Dose 10: Build Consistency — Your Reputation Depends on It

Communication excellence is not built in a single meeting but through daily credibility.

- **Be dependable:** Say what you mean and mean what you say.
- **Respond promptly and respectfully.** Delayed or careless communication erodes trust.
- **Maintain tone consistency:** Professional, courteous, and calm — regardless of context.

Over time, consistent communicators become trusted voices — and trusted voices become leaders.

Final Booster Dose: The Communicator's Oath

"I will communicate with clarity, listen with empathy, and respond with purpose —

for communication is not just a skill, but the heartbeat of leadership."

When you master the **Communication Vaccine**, you don't just exchange information — you **inspire action, build alignment, and create influence**. Every conversation then becomes a chance to strengthen your professional immunity and lead with impact.

Communication is the most powerful career vaccine.

It prevents misunderstandings, builds relationships, and amplifies your impact.

Professionals who master communication can navigate complexity, influence outcomes, and accelerate growth effortlessly.

CHAPTER 16

VISIBILITY VACCINE – PREVENTS "BEING INVISIBLE"; SHOWCASE ACHIEVEMENTS SMARTLY.

Because unrecognized contributions are career blind spots.

This vaccine ensures your **efforts and successes are seen by the right people**, enhancing influence, credibility, and growth opportunities.

The **Visibility Vaccine** is crucial for corporate career immunity because **doing great work is not enough; people must notice it smartly and strategically.**

Here's a **story** first, followed by **Prescription** for employees to cultivate this vaccine.

Story: "Rhea and the Visibility Vaccine"-*From Invisible Contributor to Recognized Leader*

Rhea joined a multinational FMCG company as a supply chain analyst. She was meticulous, always meeting deadlines and ensuring accuracy. Yet, during performance reviews, she realized she was consistently rated average, despite putting in extra effort. Her manager mentioned:

"Rhea, your work is excellent, but it often goes unnoticed. Visibility matters as much as results."

Instead of feeling demotivated, Rhea decided to take her **Visibility Vaccine**.

Steps she implemented:

1. **Documenting Achievements:** She maintained a weekly log of completed projects, improvements, and measurable outcomes.
2. **Sharing Wins Strategically:** She highlighted results in team meetings, newsletters, and dashboards without boasting — focusing on the impact rather than effort.
3. **Seeking Opportunities for Exposure:** She volunteered to present key findings to leadership and cross-functional teams.
4. **Building Relationships:** She networked with decision-makers, mentors, and project stakeholders to ensure her contributions were understood and appreciated.

Within six months, Rhea's name began circulating in leadership circles. She was nominated for a strategic project, her work received recognition at an all-hands meeting, and soon she earned her first promotion.

Rhea reflected:

"Visibility isn't about bragging; it's about ensuring your contributions create influence and open doors. The more strategically you share, the more your career immunity strengthens."

Prescription for Corporate Employees to Build the Visibility Vaccine

In today's corporate landscape, *hard work alone is not enough* — it's **visible work** that gets recognized, rewarded, and remembered. Many talented professionals fade into the background simply because they don't communicate their value effectively. The **Visibility Vaccine** strengthens your ability to be *seen, valued, and remembered* for the right reasons — with authenticity, humility, and consistency.

Here are your **10 Doses** to build sustained professional visibility and long-term career immunity.

Dose 1: Track Your Achievements — Build Your Evidence Vault

Visibility begins with clarity.

- **Maintain a personal achievement log** — note every key project, result, and measurable contribution.
- Record *metrics, client feedback, innovations,* and *problems solved* — these become your proof points during appraisals or promotions.
- Review your record monthly — this helps you articulate value effortlessly.

If you don't track your impact, you'll struggle to communicate it when it matters most.

Dose 2: Share Results, Not Just Effort

Effort earns respect; results earn recognition.

- Highlight *outcomes, efficiencies, revenue impact, or client satisfaction improvements.*
- Replace "I worked really hard" with "My work helped reduce turnaround time by 20%."
- Frame contributions in terms of *value created* — not activity completed.

Visibility grows when others can clearly see the difference you make.

Dose 3: Get Strategic About Exposure

Be intentional about where and how your work is showcased.

- **Volunteer to present** results in meetings, town halls, or team reviews.
- Offer to represent your team in *cross-functional projects* or internal newsletters.
- Look for *leadership forums* where your ideas or outcomes can gain visibility.

When opportunities don't come, create them — respectfully and strategically.

Dose 4: Network with Purpose, Not Proximity

Visibility thrives on relationships, not random encounters.

- Build connections with mentors, leaders, and peers who can notice and endorse your work.
- Stay in touch with stakeholders across departments — a wide network increases advocacy.
- Offer help, share knowledge, and be known as *a resource*, not a self-promoter.

In the visibility ecosystem, relationships are your amplifiers.

Dose 5: Celebrate Team Wins — and Subtly Spotlight Your Role

Recognition shines brightest when it's shared.

- Publicly appreciate teammates for their support and contributions.
- When discussing successes, naturally include your role ("Our analytics model that I developed improved accuracy by 15%").
- This builds trust and portrays leadership maturity.

Visibility earned through generosity creates sustainable goodwill.

Dose 6: Document and Display Impact

What gets measured gets remembered.

- Use **dashboards, visual reports, and data presentations** to make results tangible.
- Translate abstract effort into clear visuals — before-and-after comparisons, KPIs, timelines.
- Keep your documentation presentation-ready — it reinforces credibility instantly.

Your work speaks loudest when it's visual, verifiable, and valuable.

Dose 7: Be Consistent, Not Occasional

Visibility is not built in bursts — it's built through rhythm.

- Share concise monthly updates with managers or teams: key highlights, learnings, and results.
- Contribute regularly to knowledge-sharing platforms or internal communities.
- Don't vanish between review cycles — visibility fades fast in silence.

Consistency compounds — make your progress a steady pulse, not a one-time spark.

Dose 8: Seek Feedback on Your Visibility Strategy

Sometimes, your brilliance is invisible because you assume others already know.

- Ask mentors or managers directly: *"Do my contributions come across clearly to leadership?"*
- If not, recalibrate how you communicate — through reports, showcases, or cross-team updates.
- Accept suggestions on how to improve presence or influence.

🔍 *Feedback on visibility helps you see blind spots in your personal branding.*

Dose 9: Use Digital Platforms Wisely

Online visibility is your extended corporate footprint.

- Share achievements on **internal intranets, Yammer**, or **LinkedIn** thoughtfully.

- Write short insights or lessons learned — it positions you as a reflective professional.
- Celebrate milestones without boasting — let authenticity guide tone.

Digital presence multiplies visibility when paired with humility and purpose.

Dose 10: Balance Confidence with Humility

True visibility is magnetic, not noisy.

- Speak with quiet confidence about your achievements — facts, not fluff.
- Recognize team contributions and mentors who guided you.
- Avoid overexposure — people admire those who shine without overshadowing others.

Confidence earns attention; humility earns respect. Together, they build lasting influence.

Final Booster Dose: The Visibility Pledge

"I will ensure my work speaks — clearly, consistently, and collaboratively.

I will seek recognition not for vanity, but for value.

I will make visibility my vehicle for impact, not ego."

When you administer the **Visibility Vaccine**, you stop being *just another employee* and become *a visible contributor, a trusted professional, and a recognized leader-in-the-making.*

Visibility, when built with authenticity, is your career's brightest armor.

Being good is not enough; being seen strategically amplifies impact.

The Visibility Vaccine ensures your work opens doors, creates influence, and accelerates career growth — without ego or overexposure.

CHAPTER 17

INNOVATION VACCINE – KEEP CREATIVITY ALIVE IN REPETITIVE ROLES.

Because even routine tasks can become platforms for growth and recognition.

This vaccine strengthens your **ability to find creative solutions, improve processes, and add value**, ensuring your career continues to grow even in structured or repetitive roles.

The **Innovation Vaccine** is essential for corporate career immunity because it **keeps creativity alive even in repetitive or routine roles**, ensuring sustained growth and relevance.

Here's a **story** first, followed by **Prescription**.

Story: "Anil and the Innovation Vaccine"-T*urning Routine into Opportunity*

Anil joined a large logistics company as a data analyst. His role involved daily reporting and tracking KPIs — important but highly repetitive. Within a few months, he felt disengaged and worried that performing the same tasks every day would stall his career.

Instead of resigning to monotony, Anil decided to take his **Innovation Vaccine.**

Steps he implemented:

1. **Observe Patterns:** He carefully studied repetitive processes and identified bottlenecks and inefficiencies.
2. **Experiment with Ideas:** He automated simple tasks using scripts and created dashboards to reduce manual effort.
3. **Propose Improvements:** He suggested small workflow enhancements to his manager, showing measurable time savings.
4. **Explore New Perspectives:** He joined cross-functional meetings to see how his reports were used and suggested value-added insights for other teams.

The result was transformative. Anil's automation reduced reporting time by 30%, freeing him to focus on strategic analysis. Management recognized his initiative, and he was later given a project to design analytics solutions across departments — a role far more challenging and rewarding than his original position.

Reflecting on his journey, Anil said:

"Repetition doesn't kill creativity — ignoring opportunities to improve does. Innovation is a mindset, not a title."

Prescription for Corporate Employees to Build the Innovation Vaccine

In today's fast-evolving corporate world, **innovation is the immunity that protects your career from obsolescence**. Employees who consistently contribute new ideas, optimize processes, and find creative solutions are more visible, valued, and future-ready. The **Innovation Vaccine** builds your capacity to think beyond routine tasks, experiment safely, and create measurable impact. Below are your **10 Doses** for developing lasting innovation immunity.

Dose 1: Look for Pain Points — Identify Opportunities for Change

Innovation starts with observation.

- **Scan your workflows** for inefficiencies, bottlenecks, or repetitive tasks.
- **Talk to colleagues** to understand frustrations or recurring challenges in other teams.
- **Map the impact:** Identify which pain points, if solved, will bring the most value.

Every problem is a seed for innovation — spotting it early is the first dose.

Dose 2: Automate or Streamline — Reduce Manual Effort

Once pain points are identified, remove friction wherever possible.

- **Leverage tools, scripts, or templates** to simplify repetitive tasks.

- **Introduce checklists or dashboards** to reduce errors and save time.
- **Focus on efficiency gains** — even small improvements compound over time.

Automation is not just technology — it's the first step in scalable innovation.

Dose 3: Add Value Beyond Your Task

Think beyond "completing your work."

- **Consider interdependencies:** How does your task affect other teams, clients, or processes?
- **Propose insights or improvements** — not just outcomes.
- **Be solution-oriented:** Highlight what works, what doesn't, and what could be better.

Innovation grows when you connect dots outside your immediate responsibility.

Dose 4: Experiment Safely — Test Before Scaling

Innovation is as much about courage as calculation.

- **Try small pilots or prototypes** before rolling out large-scale changes.
- **Monitor results carefully** and learn from every iteration.
- **Fail fast, learn faster:** Mistakes in small doses are your strongest immunity boosters.

Safe experimentation turns ideas into validated innovations.

Dose 5: Seek Feedback — Refine Through Input

Even brilliant ideas need perspective.

- **Discuss your ideas with managers, peers, or mentors.**
- **Listen openly to constructive criticism** and adapt your approach.
- **Incorporate insights** to strengthen feasibility and adoption.

Feedback is the booster shot that transforms raw ideas into practical solutions.

Dose 6: Document Innovations — Make Impact Tangible

What isn't recorded may not be recognized.

- **Maintain a log of improvements, metrics, and results.**
- **Showcase measurable benefits** such as time saved, errors reduced, or revenue impact.
- **Use visuals or dashboards** to communicate results clearly.

Documentation not only proves value but also accelerates adoption and recognition.

Dose 7: Learn from Other Domains — Cross-Pollinate Ideas

Innovation thrives at the intersection of disciplines.

- **Observe other teams, industries, or even hobbies** for problem-solving strategies.
- **Adapt best practices** to your environment rather than reinventing the wheel.
- **Be open to unconventional sources of inspiration** — the smallest idea can trigger breakthrough solutions.

Cross-domain learning expands the palette of creative solutions.

Dose 8: Stay Curious — Continuously Explore

Curiosity is the core ingredient of innovation immunity.

- **Read books, attend webinars, or participate in professional communities.**
- **Ask "why" and "what if" questions** for every task or process.
- **Observe emerging technologies** and trends relevant to your role.

A curious mind continuously generates ideas and avoids stagnation.

Dose 9: Celebrate Small Wins — Build Momentum

Innovation is a marathon, not a sprint.

- **Recognize minor process improvements or creative solutions.**
- **Share successes with teams and leaders** to encourage replication and adoption.
- **Use micro-wins as motivation** to tackle bigger challenges.

Each small success acts as a booster dose for confidence and credibility.

Dose 10: Encourage a Culture of Innovation — Multiply the Effect

Innovation is contagious when shared.

- **Share your ideas openly** and collaborate with colleagues.
- **Mentor peers** in creative problem-solving techniques.

- **Recognize and encourage others' innovations** to build an environment of continuous improvement.

A culture of innovation strengthens immunity across the organization, creating long-term impact.

Final Booster Dose : The Innovator's Oath

"I will look beyond routine, challenge inefficiencies, experiment safely, and share solutions openly.

I will transform problems into opportunities, and ideas into impact —

making innovation not just my skill, but my career immunity."

When consistently applied, the **Innovation Vaccine** ensures you are **not just a participant, but a proactive contributor** in shaping processes, solving problems, and driving meaningful change. Innovation becomes your competitive advantage, your visibility engine, and your career shield.

Innovation isn't reserved for special roles — it's a mindset.

The Innovation Vaccine ensures that even routine work becomes a platform for learning, impact, and career acceleration.

By staying curious, proactive, and creative, employees remain indispensable and future-ready.

CHAPTER 18

STRATEGIC-THINKING VACCINE – SEE BEYOND TASKS, FOCUS ON LONG-TERM IMPACT.

Because career growth depends not only on execution but on foresight, alignment, and value creation.

This vaccine strengthens your **ability to anticipate challenges, connect actions to outcomes, and make decisions that impact long-term goals.**

The **Strategic-Thinking Vaccine** is vital for career immunity because it **transforms employees from task-doers into decision-makers who see the bigger picture and drive long-term impact.**

Here's a **story** first, followed by **prescription**.

Story: "Vikram and the Strategic-Thinking Vaccine"-*From Task-Oriented to Vision-Oriented*

Vikram joined a fast-growing consulting firm as an operations associate. He excelled at completing tasks accurately and on time, but his work was largely tactical — focusing on short-term deliverables. His manager appreciated his reliability but noted:

"Vikram, you're efficient, but I want to see how you can think beyond tasks — how your work impacts clients, revenue, and long-term strategy."

Instead of resisting, Vikram decided to take his **Strategic-Thinking Vaccine.**

Steps he implemented:

1. **Understand the Bigger Picture:** He studied the company's business model, client goals, and industry trends to understand where his work fit in.
2. **Ask 'Why' Beyond Tasks:** For every task, he asked, *"How does this affect outcomes? What is the long-term impact?"*
3. **Propose Forward-Looking Solutions:** He suggested process improvements and small initiatives that aligned with business growth.
4. **Collaborate Across Teams:** He worked with sales, marketing, and finance to ensure his projects supported broader objectives.

Over time, Vikram's perspective shifted from doing tasks to **solving problems strategically.** Leadership noticed, and he was entrusted with leading a project that directly influenced a major client strategy. His ability to connect day-to-day work with long-term outcomes accelerated his promotion and recognition.

Reflecting on his journey, Vikram said:

"Tasks are important, but strategy is transformational. When you see the bigger picture, your contributions multiply — and so does your career trajectory."

Prescription for Corporate Employees to Build the Strategic-Thinking Vaccine

Strategic thinking is the **immune system of your career**, helping you anticipate change, align actions with organizational goals, and deliver impact that goes beyond immediate tasks. Employees who master strategic thinking are **proactive, high-value contributors** — they see patterns, connect dots, and influence decisions effectively. The **Strategic-Thinking Vaccine** strengthens your ability to navigate complexity, anticipate outcomes, and position yourself as a long-term asset. Below are your **10 Doses** for cultivating strategic thinking immunity.

Dose 1: Understand the Organization and Industry — Map the Landscape

Strategic thinking begins with knowledge.

- **Learn the business model:** How does your company generate revenue, deliver value, and differentiate itself?
- **Study key clients and competitors:** Understand market positioning, challenges, and opportunities.
- **Observe industry trends:** Stay aware of regulatory changes, emerging technologies, and customer expectations.

A deep understanding of the ecosystem provides the context for informed decisions.

Dose 2: Ask Big-Picture Questions — Connect Actions to Impact

Every task has a purpose — your job is to uncover it.

- **Question the "why":** For each assignment, ask: "How does this contribute to revenue, efficiency, or strategic goals?"
- **Challenge assumptions:** Look beyond instructions to see underlying objectives.
- **Think long-term:** Immediate outputs matter, but strategic outcomes define career impact.

Strategic thinkers always see the forest, not just the trees.

Dose 3: Connect Dots Across Teams — Build a Holistic View

Complex problems rarely exist in isolation.

- **Collaborate across functions:** Understand dependencies between teams, systems, and processes.
- **Leverage synergies:** Identify where collaboration can create efficiency or innovation.
- **Observe interconnections:** Recognize how decisions in one area ripple across the organization.

Strategic insight comes from seeing relationships others overlook.

Dose 4: Prioritize High-Impact Work — Focus on What Matters Most

Time and energy are finite — use them wisely.

- **Identify high-value initiatives:** Focus on tasks that create long-term business impact.

- **Avoid busywork traps:** Not every task deserves the same attention — learn to say no strategically.
- **Evaluate ROI:** Ask, "Will this effort move the needle for the organization?"

Strategic thinkers allocate effort where it multiplies results.

Dose 5: Think in Scenarios — Anticipate Risks and Opportunities

Preparation is the core of strategic immunity.

- **Consider multiple approaches:** Analyze potential risks, rewards, and unintended consequences.
- **Visualize outcomes:** What happens if you succeed, fail, or encounter resistance?
- **Prepare contingency plans:** The best strategies include options for changing circumstances.

Scenario planning converts uncertainty into calculated opportunity.

Dose 6: Propose Forward-Looking Solutions — Think Beyond Today

Strategy is about shaping the future, not just managing the present.

- **Identify improvements:** Streamline processes, reduce bottlenecks, or optimize client interactions.
- **Anticipate needs:** Predict challenges before they become urgent.
- **Offer practical, scalable solutions:** Ideas gain traction when they balance innovation with feasibility.

Strategic thinkers influence outcomes rather than just reacting to them.

Dose 7: Track Outcomes — Measure Impact Consistently

Insight without evidence is incomplete.

- **Measure the results:** Monitor KPIs, team performance, or client satisfaction.
- **Analyze trends:** Understand what worked, what didn't, and why.
- **Adjust strategy:** Use data to refine decisions and improve future initiatives.

Metrics provide proof of strategic effectiveness and build credibility.

Dose 8: Learn from Leaders — Observe Strategic Patterns

Leadership is a live case study in strategic thinking.

- **Watch decision-making:** How do senior managers connect daily operations to long-term goals?
- **Analyze prioritization:** Notice how they balance competing demands and risks.
- **Emulate approaches:** Adapt successful strategies to your level and role.

Leaders' patterns offer a template for your own strategic development.

Dose 9: Reflect Regularly — Internalize Lessons

Strategy grows through conscious reflection.

- **Review weekly:** Which actions contributed to long-term objectives? Which were reactive?
- **Identify gaps:** Notice missed opportunities or unaligned efforts.
- **Plan improvements:** Use reflection to prioritize future strategic initiatives.

Regular reflection turns experience into foresight.

Dose 10: Mentor Others — Reinforce Strategic Thinking

Teaching is the ultimate booster for strategy immunity.

- **Share frameworks:** Help teammates connect tasks to organizational objectives.
- **Discuss scenarios:** Encourage colleagues to think ahead and anticipate consequences.
- **Provide guidance:** Mentoring strengthens your influence and embeds strategic thinking in your team.

Strategic thinking multiplies when shared — benefiting both you and your organization.

Final Booster Dose: The Strategic Thinker's Pledge

"I will see beyond my tasks, connect dots across functions, anticipate outcomes, and prioritize high-impact actions.

I will convert data into insight, insight into action, and action into measurable impact.

I will not just work — I will think strategically to shape the future."

When consistently applied, the **Strategic-Thinking Vaccine** ensures that you **are not only executing tasks but influencing direction, making decisions that matter, and positioning yourself as a trusted, forward-looking professional.**

Execution gets you noticed, strategy gets you ahead.

The Strategic-Thinking Vaccine ensures you see beyond immediate tasks, influence outcomes, and position yourself as a leader.

Professionals who cultivate strategic thinking remain indispensable and future-ready, immune to career stagnation.

CHAPTER 19

PERSONAL-BRANDING VACCINE – BUILD A UNIQUE IDENTITY BEYOND YOUR DESIGNATION.

Because how others perceive your impact often determines career growth more than your job title.

This vaccine strengthens your **visibility, reputation, and influence**, making your skills, values, and achievements recognized independently of your current role.

The **Personal-Branding Vaccine** is crucial for career immunity because it **ensures that your reputation, skills, and impact are recognized, remembered, and associated with value beyond your current role.**

Here's a **story** first, followed by **Prescription** for employees.

Story: "Simran and the Personal-Branding Vaccine"- Becoming More Than a Job Title

Simran joined a multinational consulting firm as a business analyst. She was diligent and competent, completing tasks efficiently. However, she noticed that despite her good work, opportunities often went to others who were more visible or recognized in leadership circles.

Determined not to be just another "faceless contributor," Simran decided to take her **Personal-Branding Vaccine.**

Steps she implemented:

1. **Define Her Unique Value:** She identified her strengths — analytical skills, problem-solving, and creative presentations — and thought about how to consistently showcase them.
2. **Create a Signature Style:** She consistently applied structured, visually appealing reports and presentations that became recognizable to clients and leadership.
3. **Network Strategically:** She built relationships across departments and shared her insights in cross-functional forums.
4. **Share Knowledge Publicly:** She contributed to internal newsletters, blogs, and learning sessions, positioning herself as an expert in her domain.
5. **Seek Opportunities Beyond Designation:** She volunteered for special projects, workshops, and mentoring initiatives that leveraged her strengths.

Within a year, Simran's reputation grew. Colleagues, managers, and clients associated her name with quality, reliability, and innovation. When a leadership position opened, she was considered first, not just because of experience, but because of her **distinct personal brand.**

Reflecting on her journey, Simran said:

"Your designation is temporary; your brand is permanent. Cultivate it consciously, and it will open doors that titles cannot."

Prescription for Corporate Employees to Build the Personal-Branding Vaccine

In today's corporate environment, talent alone is no longer enough. **Personal branding is your professional immune system** — it ensures that your skills, achievements, and unique value are recognized, remembered, and trusted. The **Personal-Branding Vaccine** helps you craft a reputation that is authentic, visible, and aligned with your career ambitions. Below are your **10 Doses** for cultivating a strong personal brand.

Dose 1: Identify Your Unique Value Proposition — Know Your Differentiator

Your personal brand starts with clarity about what sets you apart.

- **Assess your strengths:** Skills, expertise, experiences, or perspectives that differentiate you from peers.
- **Highlight your niche:** Are you a problem-solver, relationship-builder, strategist, or innovator?
- **Frame it in value terms:** How do your unique qualities contribute to team and organizational success?

Clarity on your unique value lays the foundation for a visible, respected brand.

Dose 2: Be Consistent — Reinforce Your Identity

A brand is built on repeated impressions.

- **Apply your strengths consistently** in daily work, meetings, and interactions.
- **Show up with reliability:** Let your expertise and professionalism define how others experience you.
- **Avoid mixed signals:** Your actions, words, and outputs should all communicate the same value.

Consistency transforms skills into a trusted reputation.

Dose 3: Deliver Quality with Impact — Let Work Speak

Excellence is the core of personal branding.

- **Focus on outcomes:** Make your work measurable, meaningful, and memorable.
- **Seek visibility:** Present results in reports, dashboards, or team discussions.
- **Go beyond completion:** Solve problems creatively, anticipate needs, and exceed expectations.

High-quality output is the strongest proof of your brand's value.

Dose 4: Network Across Levels — Expand Your Sphere of Influence

Personal branding thrives on relationships.

- **Connect with peers, seniors, and stakeholders** beyond your immediate team.
- **Understand others' priorities:** Tailor your interactions to show relevance and value.
- **Be known as reliable and collaborative:** Visibility increases when your network advocates for you.

A strong network amplifies recognition and opens career opportunities.

Dose 5: Share Knowledge — Position Yourself as a Resource

Influence grows when you teach and contribute.

- **Participate in internal presentations, training sessions, or newsletters.**
- **Mentor peers or juniors:** Sharing expertise reinforces authority and credibility.
- **Document and share insights:** Make yourself the go-to person in your domain.

Knowledge-sharing converts competence into influence.

Dose 6: Communicate Your Wins Strategically — Show Value Without Boasting

Recognition comes when achievements are visible and contextualized.

- **Frame wins with impact:** Focus on results, improvements, or value created rather than effort alone.
- **Share selectively:** Highlight achievements with relevance to audience and objectives.

- **Balance confidence with humility:** Let results speak, supported by professional articulation.

Strategic communication makes your contributions memorable without appearing self-serving.

Dose 7: Maintain a Professional Online Presence — Amplify Your Brand Digitally

Digital presence is the modern extension of your personal brand.

- **Keep LinkedIn or industry platforms updated:** Share insights, projects, and accomplishments.
- **Demonstrate thought leadership:** Write posts, articles, or comment meaningfully in your domain.
- **Engage authentically:** Participate in discussions, acknowledge others' contributions, and add value.

A professional online footprint multiplies visibility beyond your immediate organization.

Dose 8: Seek Feedback — Refine and Strengthen Your Brand

Perception shapes reputation.

- **Ask mentors, peers, and managers:** How do they perceive your strengths, reliability, and impact?
- **Listen actively:** Accept constructive criticism and implement changes thoughtfully.
- **Iterate your brand:** Adjust messaging, behavior, and focus to align with feedback.

Feedback acts as a booster, ensuring your brand remains authentic and effective.

Dose 9: Align Brand with Career Goals — Ensure Directional Consistency

A brand without alignment can confuse others.

- **Define your long-term ambitions:** Leadership, innovation, domain expertise, or global exposure.
- **Position your brand to reflect desired trajectory:** Tailor projects, skills, and communications accordingly.
- **Review periodically:** Ensure your actions and messaging continue to reinforce the career path you aspire to.

Alignment ensures your personal brand accelerates, not distracts from, your goals.

Dose 10: Be Authentic — Sustainability Comes from Genuineness

True influence cannot be faked.

- **Reflect your genuine strengths, values, and passions** in all interactions.
- **Avoid over-curation or exaggeration:** Authenticity attracts trust and long-term respect.
- **Let personality complement professionalism:** People connect with humans, not just resumes.

An authentic personal brand grows naturally and sustains over time.

Final Booster Dose: The Personal-Branding Pledge

"I will identify and consistently showcase my unique value.

I will communicate achievements strategically, share knowledge generously, and maintain authenticity in all professional interactions.

I will build a brand that reflects my strengths, my impact, and my aspirations — making me visible, valued, and trusted in every context."

When consistently applied, the **Personal-Branding Vaccine** ensures that you are **recognized for your value, remembered for your contributions, and positioned as a future-ready professional** — all while staying true to yourself.

Your designation is temporary; your personal brand is permanent.

The Personal-Branding Vaccine ensures that your reputation, skills, and influence travel with you, giving your career immunity against being overlooked, undervalued, or stagnating.

Professionals who build a strong personal brand are noticed, trusted, and chosen for opportunities — even before applying.

CHAPTER 20

COLLABORATION VACCINE – CREATES IMMUNITY AGAINST SILOS & "LONE WOLF SYNDROME."

Because isolated efforts, no matter how excellent, rarely achieve lasting impact.

This vaccine strengthens your **ability to work across teams, leverage collective strengths, and create synergy**, ensuring higher performance, visibility, and long-term career growth.

The **Collaboration Vaccine** is essential for career immunity because it **ensures employees thrive in teams, avoid isolation, and maximize impact by working synergistically across functions.**

Here's a **story** first, followed by **Prescription**.

Story: "Rahul and the Collaboration Vaccine"-*From Lone Wolf to Team Leader*

Rahul joined a global IT company as a software developer. He was highly skilled and preferred working independently. While his individual output was excellent, his projects often faced integration challenges because he rarely coordinated with other teams.

During a major project, delays occurred due to misalignment between development, QA, and client services. His manager pointed out:

"Rahul, your work is great individually, but the project needs teamwork. Collaboration is as important as coding."

Instead of resisting, Rahul decided to take his **Collaboration Vaccine**.

Steps he implemented:

1. **Engage Early:** He started involving other teams from project inception, understanding their workflows and constraints.
2. **Share Knowledge:** He conducted short knowledge-sharing sessions to align everyone on technical decisions.
3. **Communicate Transparently:** Rahul maintained clear updates and encouraged feedback to avoid misunderstandings.
4. **Leverage Strengths:** He identified complementary skills in teammates and delegated tasks strategically rather than doing everything himself.

The outcome was transformative. Projects ran smoothly, timelines improved, and Rahul's reputation shifted from "solo expert" to a **trusted collaborative leader**. Leadership recognized him for cross-functional effectiveness and later promoted him to lead a multi-team project.

Reflecting on his journey, Rahul said:

"Collaboration doesn't dilute your contribution — it amplifies it. The more you work with others, the stronger and broader your impact."

Prescription for Corporate Employees to Build the Collaboration Vaccine

Collaboration is the **immune system that protects your career from isolation and redundancy**. In today's interconnected corporate ecosystem, the ability to work seamlessly across teams, functions, and hierarchies is not optional — it's essential. The **Collaboration Vaccine** equips employees with the mindset, skills, and behaviors to contribute effectively in group settings, build trust, and amplify impact. Below are your **10 Doses** for developing robust collaboration immunity.

Dose 1: Engage Proactively — Involve the Right People Early

Collaboration begins before work starts.

- **Identify stakeholders:** Map out who will be affected by or can influence the project.
- **Engage early:** Align expectations, clarify responsibilities, and anticipate concerns.
- **Set clear goals together:** Early engagement reduces misalignment and builds shared ownership.

Proactivity ensures collaboration is strategic, not reactive.

Dose 2: Share Knowledge — Build Trust Through Transparency

Information is the currency of collaboration.

- **Offer insights freely:** Share expertise, data, or solutions without waiting to be asked.
- **Document and distribute learnings:** Meeting notes, process guides, or lessons learned help the entire team.
- **Encourage a culture of openness:** Knowledge-sharing fosters trust and reduces redundancy.

Teams collaborate best when knowledge flows freely and consistently.

Dose 3: Communicate Clearly — Maintain Transparency

Miscommunication is collaboration's biggest enemy.

- **Provide regular updates:** Keep team members informed of progress, challenges, and changes.
- **Clarify assumptions:** Avoid hidden silos by discussing expectations and responsibilities openly.
- **Use structured communication tools:** Emails, dashboards, and status meetings create shared understanding.

Clear communication prevents friction and builds credibility across teams.

Dose 4: Leverage Complementary Skills — Optimize Team Strengths

Collaboration thrives when each member contributes their best.

- **Identify strengths:** Assess skills, experience, and working styles of teammates.
- **Distribute tasks strategically:** Match responsibilities to individual strengths for efficiency and quality.
- **Encourage cross-learning:** Complementary skillsets enhance collective performance.

A team that plays to its strengths achieves far more than the sum of its parts.

Dose 5: Seek Feedback — Integrate Diverse Perspectives

Collaboration is iterative, not linear.

- **Encourage suggestions:** Ask team members for input on decisions, processes, or solutions.
- **Listen actively:** Validate ideas, weigh perspectives, and integrate feedback where feasible.
- **Adapt accordingly:** Flexibility in response to input strengthens team cohesion.

Feedback is a booster that refines solutions and reinforces trust.

Dose 6: Build Cross-Functional Relationships — Expand Your Influence

Collaboration extends beyond immediate teams.

- **Network across departments:** Understand how other functions operate and contribute.
- **Develop rapport with peers in different areas:** This facilitates smoother workflows and quicker approvals.

- **Recognize interdependencies:** Appreciate how collaborative success impacts organizational objectives.

Cross-functional relationships multiply influence and create allies across the company.

Dose 7: Celebrate Team Wins — Reinforce Collective Success

Recognition strengthens bonds.

- **Acknowledge contributions:** Highlight teammates' roles in achieving outcomes.
- **Communicate impact:** Demonstrate how the collective effort benefited the project or organization.
- **Balance visibility:** Subtlely highlight your contributions while emphasizing teamwork.

Celebrating wins builds morale, trust, and a collaborative culture.

Dose 8: Resolve Conflicts Constructively — Turn Tension into Growth

Disagreements are inevitable — resolution is key.

- **Address issues openly:** Discuss disagreements respectfully and promptly.
- **Focus on solutions:** Move past blame to identify compromises or corrective measures.
- **Maintain neutrality:** Be a facilitator, not a partisan, to keep collaboration healthy.

Constructive conflict management strengthens team resilience and cohesion.

Dose 9: Be Flexible — Adapt to People and Contexts

Every team and project has unique dynamics.

- **Adjust working style:** Adapt to cultural norms, communication preferences, and project demands.
- **Embrace role fluidity:** Be willing to step into new responsibilities when needed.
- **Balance assertiveness with receptivity:** Know when to lead and when to support.

Flexibility ensures collaboration thrives despite differences in style or perspective.

Dose 10: Model Collaborative Behavior — Lead by Example

Behavior is contagious — set the standard.

- **Demonstrate cooperation:** Show patience, transparency, and reliability in interactions.
- **Mentor others in teamwork:** Encourage juniors to adopt collaborative practices.
- **Reinforce culture:** Your consistent example encourages peers to mirror positive behaviors.

Leading by example embeds collaboration into the team's DNA and organizational culture.

Final Booster Dose: The Collaborator's Pledge

"I will proactively engage with stakeholders, share knowledge generously, communicate transparently, and leverage collective strengths.

I will seek diverse perspectives, celebrate team success, resolve conflicts constructively, and adapt to every situation.

I will model collaborative behavior to strengthen my team and the organization, making collaboration my career immunity."

No career flourishes in isolation.

The Collaboration Vaccine ensures that your skills, influence, and impact are amplified through teamwork.

Professionals who cultivate collaboration avoid silos, accelerate project success, and become indispensable contributors and leaders.

CHAPTER 21

DELEGATION VACCINE – PROTECTS FROM OVERWORK AND MICROMANAGEMENT.

Because doing everything yourself limits your growth and exhausts your energy.

This vaccine strengthens your **ability to assign tasks effectively, empower others, and focus on high-value responsibilities**, protecting your time, energy, and career trajectory.

The **Delegation Vaccine** is essential for career immunity because it **prevents burnout, boosts productivity, and positions you as a trusted leader by leveraging team strengths effectively.**

Here's a **story** first, followed by **Prescription**.

Story: "Nisha and the Delegation Vaccine"-*From Overworked to Empowered Leader*

Nisha joined a fast-growing marketing firm as a project manager. She prided herself on doing everything perfectly and often ended up handling both strategic planning and execution tasks herself. Within a few months, she was overworked, stressed, and unable to focus on high-impact decisions.

During a leadership review, her manager observed:

"Nisha, your dedication is admirable, but you're spending too much time on tasks others can handle. Learning to delegate is key to scaling your impact."

Determined to change, Nisha decided to take her **Delegation Vaccine**.

Steps she implemented:

1. **Identify Tasks to Delegate:** She listed repetitive or lower-priority tasks that others could handle.
2. **Choose the Right People:** She matched tasks to team members based on skills, capacity, and growth opportunities.
3. **Provide Clear Instructions:** Nisha set expectations, shared context, and defined desired outcomes.
4. **Empower and Trust:** She avoided micromanaging, allowed autonomy, and provided support only when necessary.
5. **Follow Up Strategically:** She monitored progress through updates rather than constant oversight.

The results were immediate. Team productivity improved, deadlines were met efficiently, and Nisha could focus on strategic initiatives, client relationships, and leadership decisions. Her team members also felt more valued and motivated. Within six months, Nisha was recognized for her leadership skills and promoted to senior project manager.

Reflecting on her journey, Nisha said:

"Delegation isn't just about offloading work — it's about multiplying impact. When you trust your team, everyone grows, including you."

Prescription for Corporate Employees to Build the Delegation Vaccine

Delegation is **the career immunity booster that multiplies your impact**. It allows you to focus on strategic priorities while developing your team's skills and accountability. The **Delegation Vaccine** ensures that you are not overburdened by tasks, while simultaneously empowering others and strengthening organizational effectiveness. Below is the **10-Dose Prescription** for mastering delegation.

Dose 1: Identify Core vs. Non-Core Tasks — Prioritize for Maximum Impact

Delegation starts with clarity on what truly requires your expertise.

- **Analyze your workload:** Separate high-value, strategic responsibilities from routine, repetitive, or low-priority tasks.
- **Focus your energy:** Invest time in tasks that directly influence goals, client outcomes, or leadership visibility.

- **Delegate the rest:** Routine tasks become opportunities for team development rather than drains on your bandwidth.

🎯 *Prioritization ensures your time and energy are leveraged for maximum professional impact.*

Dose 2: Choose the Right People — Align Tasks with Skills and Growth

Effective delegation depends on matching work to the right hands.

- **Assess capabilities:** Consider skills, experience, interests, and development goals of team members.
- **Distribute strategically:** Assign tasks that challenge, stretch, or strengthen competencies.
- **Promote ownership:** Empowering the right person fosters accountability and confidence.

Skillful matching transforms tasks into growth opportunities for your team.

Dose 3: Set Clear Expectations — Define Outcomes Upfront

Ambiguity is the enemy of delegation.

- **Clarify goals:** Explain what success looks like and why it matters.
- **Specify deadlines and quality standards:** Reduce confusion and prevent repeated corrections.
- **Outline deliverables:** Use clear documentation or templates where necessary.

Transparent expectations prevent misunderstandings and increase efficiency.

Dose 4: Provide Context, Not Micromanagement — Inspire Understanding

Delegation works best when the "why" is understood.

- **Explain the bigger picture:** Show how the task aligns with team objectives, projects, or organizational strategy.
- **Empower decision-making:** Provide boundaries but avoid controlling every detail.
- **Encourage initiative:** Context fosters critical thinking and ownership.

People perform better when they understand the purpose behind their actions.

Dose 5: Trust Your Team — Step Back to Let Them Lead

Autonomy is essential for skill development.

- **Resist overchecking:** Avoid monitoring every minor step.
- **Allow ownership:** Let team members make decisions and learn from outcomes.
- **Build confidence:** Trust strengthens accountability and encourages innovation.

Trust is the immunity booster that turns delegation into team empowerment.

Dose 6: Offer Support, Not Control — Be Available Without Overstepping

Delegation requires the right balance of guidance.

- **Be a resource:** Offer advice, mentorship, or clarification when needed.
- **Avoid taking over:** Let mistakes happen safely; they are learning opportunities.
- **Encourage problem-solving:** Prompt solutions instead of providing answers immediately.

Supportive guidance reinforces confidence and independence in your team.

Dose 7: Monitor Progress Strategically — Check Without Micromanaging

Visibility ensures accountability without creating dependency.

- **Use updates or dashboards:** Track progress efficiently.
- **Schedule brief check-ins:** Focus on problem-solving rather than step-by-step control.
- **Identify roadblocks early:** Provide help proactively but maintain autonomy.

Strategic monitoring balances oversight with empowerment.

Dose 8: Give Credit — Recognize Contributions Publicly

Acknowledgment strengthens motivation and trust.

- **Highlight team achievements:** Celebrate individual and collective efforts.

- **Tie recognition to outcomes:** Show how their contributions impacted results.
- **Reinforce accountability:** Public acknowledgment encourages future initiative-taking.

Giving credit nurtures a high-performing, collaborative team culture.

Dose 9: Reflect and Adjust — Learn from Every Delegation

Continuous improvement ensures mastery.

- **Evaluate outcomes:** Identify what worked well and what could be refined.
- **Assess team readiness:** Determine if more training or clarity is needed next time.
- **Apply lessons to future tasks:** Iterative learning enhances both your delegation and leadership skills.

Reflection turns each delegated project into a booster dose for personal and team growth.

Dose 10: Scale Your Impact — Free Yourself for Strategic Leadership

Delegation multiplies your influence across the organization.

- **Focus on strategy and innovation:** Freed from routine tasks, you can tackle higher-value initiatives.
- **Develop future leaders:** Delegation creates a capable team ready for bigger responsibilities.
- **Expand reach:** The more effectively you delegate, the greater your organizational impact.

Delegation transforms individual effort into collective achievement and positions you as a strategic leader.

Final Booster Dose: The Delegator's Pledge

"I will identify tasks worthy of my focus and delegate the rest to capable team members.

I will provide context, set clear expectations, trust my team, and offer guidance without control.

I will recognize contributions, reflect on outcomes, and continuously refine my delegation approach.

Through effective delegation, I multiply impact, empower others, and free myself to lead strategically."

Delegation is the multiplier of impact.

The Delegation Vaccine ensures you avoid burnout, empower your team, and focus on work that truly advances your career.

Leaders who delegate effectively grow themselves and those around them, creating a high-performing, resilient team.

CHAPTER 22

OPPORTUNITY-SEEKING VACCINE – SPOT HIDDEN CHANCES FOR GROWTH.

Because waiting passively limits your career, while proactive pursuit multiplies chances for learning, recognition, and advancement.

This vaccine strengthens your **ability to anticipate, identify, and act on growth opportunities**, giving you a decisive edge in career progression.

The **Opportunity-Seeking Vaccine** is a career booster because it **teaches employees to proactively identify hidden chances for growth, learning, and recognition** rather than waiting for opportunities to appear.

Here's a **story** first, followed by **Prescription.**

Story: "Amit and the Opportunity-Seeking Vaccine"- *Finding Gold Where Others Walk Past*

Amit joined a mid-sized IT consulting firm as a junior analyst. He completed assigned tasks diligently but noticed that promotions and high-visibility projects often went to colleagues who seemed more "in the right place at the right time."

Instead of being passive, Amit decided to take his **Opportunity-Seeking Vaccine**.

Steps he implemented:

1. **Scan the Environment:** Amit regularly monitored internal announcements, client updates, and leadership conversations for potential projects or skill gaps.
2. **Volunteer for Stretch Assignments:** When he saw a new client pilot project that needed extra support, he proactively offered help, even though it wasn't in his job description.
3. **Build Early Relationships:** Amit connected with project leads, mentors, and peers to understand where help was needed most.
4. **Pitch Value-Add Ideas:** He proposed small but meaningful improvements in existing processes, demonstrating initiative.

The outcome was transformational. Amit was assigned to a high-profile client project, gained new skills, and built visibility across leadership teams. Within a year, he became a preferred choice for strategic projects, accelerating his career growth.

Reflecting on his journey, Amit said:

"Opportunities don't always knock — sometimes you need to spot the open window and step through it. Career immunity comes from being alert, proactive, and ready to act."

Prescription for Corporate Employees to Build the Opportunity-Seeking Vaccine

Opportunities are **the career boosters that accelerate growth, visibility, and leadership readiness.** The **Opportunity-Seeking Vaccine** equips professionals to stay alert, identify high-impact openings, and act decisively to leverage them — turning potential into measurable results. Below is the **10-Dose Prescription** for developing a robust opportunity-seeking immunity.

Dose 1: Stay Alert — Cultivate Situational Awareness

Opportunity rarely announces itself.

- **Scan the environment continuously:** Pay attention to internal announcements, team meetings, emails, and informal hallway conversations.
- **Tune into trends:** Monitor organizational priorities, project pipelines, and emerging client needs.
- **Listen actively:** Often, opportunities are hinted at in casual discussions rather than formal calls.

Awareness primes you to recognize openings before others even notice them.

Dose 2: Look Beyond Your Job Description — Think Horizontally

Your role is a platform, not a cage.

- **Identify cross-functional value-adds:** Consider tasks where your skills can benefit other teams or projects.
- **Stretch your scope:** Take initiative in areas outside your current mandate without overstepping authority.

- **Observe pain points:** Where processes falter or gaps exist, your contribution can stand out.

Opportunity often hides just beyond the edges of your defined responsibilities.

Dose 3: Volunteer for Stretch Assignments — Step Into the Arena

Growth begins where comfort ends.

- **Seek challenging projects:** Target assignments that require skills you're developing or have yet to showcase.
- **Demonstrate leadership potential:** Tackling complex tasks signals readiness for higher responsibility.
- **Accept risk mindfully:** Even if results are imperfect, visibility and learning are invaluable.

Stretch assignments act as live inoculations — building confidence and resilience.

Dose 4: Network with Purpose — Connect to Hidden Doors

Relationships are the conduits to opportunity.

- **Identify key influencers:** Build rapport with mentors, senior leaders, and cross-functional colleagues.
- **Engage authentically:** Seek insights, share ideas, and maintain meaningful connections.
- **Stay visible:** Be known as someone proactive and capable, so opportunities are naturally referred to you.

Networking transforms information into actionable openings.

Dose 5: Observe Gaps and Needs — Become a Problem Finder

Opportunities emerge where gaps exist.

- **Scan processes and workflows:** Look for inefficiencies or bottlenecks.
- **Monitor client or market needs:** Identify areas where your team can add value.
- **Suggest solutions proactively:** Be the person who brings both problems and answers to the table.

Spotting unmet needs positions you as a solution-oriented professional, ready for advancement.

Dose 6: Pitch Ideas Strategically — Transform Insight into Action

Ideas alone are not enough; timing and framing matter.

- **Align proposals with objectives:** Ensure your suggestions contribute to business goals or key metrics.
- **Be concise and evidence-backed:** Present clear rationale, anticipated outcomes, and implementation steps.
- **Choose the right forum:** Share ideas in team meetings, with mentors, or directly with decision-makers.

Strategic pitching converts recognition into real opportunities.

Dose 7: Be Ready and Prepared — Build Skills in Anticipation

Opportunities favor the prepared mind.

- **Maintain a learning mindset:** Continuously develop relevant skills, knowledge, and competencies.

- **Create "ready-to-act" capability:** Build templates, frameworks, or tools that allow quick action.
- **Simulate scenarios:** Anticipate challenges and rehearse responses for high-stakes opportunities.

Preparation allows you to seize openings confidently and credibly.

Dose 8: Track Opportunities — Keep a Personal Opportunity Log

Clarity accelerates follow-through.

- **Maintain a record:** Note potential projects, desired roles, and skills needed.
- **Prioritize strategically:** Identify opportunities that align with long-term goals and immediate growth.
- **Monitor progress:** Update your log with actions taken, outcomes, and lessons learned.

Tracking ensures no opportunity slips through the cracks and builds situational memory.

Dose 9: Follow Through — Convert Potential into Results

Action converts observation into achievement.

- **Act decisively:** Once an opportunity is identified, commit fully to execution.
- **Deliver measurable outcomes:** Demonstrate tangible impact through results and metrics.
- **Seek feedback:** Learn what worked and how to improve for next time.

Follow-through strengthens credibility and multiplies future opportunities.

Dose 10: Reflect and Learn — Strengthen Your Opportunity Radar

Post-action reflection enhances immunity.

- **Analyze successes and misses:** Identify patterns of opportunities that yield growth versus those that do not.
- **Refine detection skills:** Recognize early signs of high-value opportunities faster.
- **Document lessons:** Maintain a personal record of insights and strategies for future use.

Reflection sharpens judgment and primes you for continuous opportunity-seeking.

Final Booster Dose : The Opportunity-Seeker's Pledge

"I will remain vigilant to emerging possibilities, look beyond my immediate role, and proactively seek stretch assignments.

I will nurture purposeful relationships, observe unmet needs, pitch solutions strategically, and prepare myself to act decisively.

I will track opportunities, follow through with impact, and reflect on each experience to sharpen my future vision.

Through these actions, I convert potential into achievement, ensuring sustained growth, visibility, and career immunity."

Opportunities favor the proactive, not the passive.

The Opportunity-Seeking Vaccine ensures you don't just react to career openings — you anticipate, identify, and act on hidden chances for growth.

Professionals who cultivate this vaccine stay ahead, accelerate learning, and consistently position themselves for success.

Career Vaccines – Executive Leadership & Career Longevity

After mastering core skills and building visibility, influence, and strategic thinking, the final set of vaccines prepares you for **executive-level roles**. These doses enhance decision-making, empathy, crisis management, influence, cultural intelligence, and long-term sustainability — the hallmarks of senior leadership.

C. Longevity Vaccines (Immunity – Senior Level)

CHAPTER 23

DECISION-MAKING VACCINE – IMMUNITY AGAINST OVERTHINKING PARALYSIS.

Because hesitation and over analysis stall career growth, while timely decisions drive influence and advancement.

This vaccine strengthens your **ability to analyze, decide, act, and adapt**, ensuring managers are recognized as trusted leaders capable of handling complexity at executive levels.

The **Decision-Making Vaccine** is a must-have for managers aiming to rise to executive levels, because **executives are valued for clarity, speed, and impact of decisions, not just ideas.**

Here's a **story** first, followed by **prescription** for managers seeking career immunity and executive growth.

Story: "Neha and the Decision-Making Vaccine"- *From Hesitant Manager to Executive Leader*

Neha was a mid-level operations manager at a multinational manufacturing firm. She was competent, diligent, and highly respected by her team. However, when faced with complex, ambiguous decisions — like resource allocation, vendor selection, or cross-departmental priorities — she often overanalyzed options and delayed action.

During a performance review, her director remarked:

"Neha, your team trusts you, but to move to an executive role, you need to make timely decisions even under uncertainty. Overthinking slows growth and reduces impact."

Determined to advance, Neha decided to take her **Decision-Making Vaccine**.

Steps she implemented:

1. **Clarify Objectives:** She focused on the key outcomes and metrics before evaluating options.
2. **Limit Options:** Instead of considering every possible alternative, she shortlisted the top 2–3 viable options.
3. **Gather Key Data Quickly:** She prioritized essential information and avoided analysis paralysis.
4. **Act Decisively:** Once a decision was made, she implemented it confidently and monitored outcomes.
5. **Learn and Adapt:** She treated every decision as a learning opportunity, adjusting strategies based on results.

Over time, Neha's speed and clarity in decision-making became her hallmark. Leadership trusted her with high-stakes projects, cross-functional budgets, and strategic initiatives. Within two years, she was promoted to director, and later positioned herself as a candidate for executive leadership.

Reflecting on her journey, Neha said:

"Executives aren't perfect decision-makers; they are decisive ones. Timely, informed action creates momentum and trust."

Prescription for Corporate Managers to Build the Decision-Making Vaccine

Decision-making is **the executive immunity booster** — the ability to assess complex situations, act decisively, and generate impactful results. The **Decision-Making Vaccine** equips managers with the cognitive clarity, strategic foresight, and confidence to make choices that propel teams, projects, and organizations forward. Below is the **10-Dose Prescription** for cultivating robust decision-making immunity.

Dose 1: Focus on Outcomes, Not Perfection — Think Impact, Not Details

Effective decisions prioritize results over trivialities.

- **Define the end goal:** Clearly articulate the desired business or project outcome before diving into options.
- **Avoid overanalyzing minutiae:** Not every decision demands exhaustive research; discern what matters most.

- **Align with organizational objectives:** Ensure your decisions contribute meaningfully to strategy, revenue, or efficiency.

Outcome-oriented thinking keeps decisions aligned with value creation rather than endless perfection-seeking.

Dose 2: Prioritize Decisions — Tackle What Matters Most

Not every choice carries equal weight.

- **Identify high-impact decisions:** Focus your energy on choices that affect revenue, client satisfaction, team performance, or long-term strategy.
- **Defer or delegate low-stakes decisions:** Routine or operational matters should not distract you from critical ones.
- **Assess urgency vs. importance:** Use frameworks like the Eisenhower Matrix to structure decision priority.

Prioritization ensures energy is invested where it produces maximum return.

Dose 3: Limit Options — Prevent Analysis Paralysis

Too many choices can stall action.

- **Shortlist 2–3 viable alternatives:** Avoid endless brainstorming that delays progress.
- **Focus on feasible solutions:** Assess options against resources, timelines, and risk tolerance.
- **Recognize diminishing returns:** Excessive alternatives rarely improve outcomes significantly.

Option-limiting is a protective booster against indecision and delayed execution.

Dose 4: Gather Essential Data Only — Avoid Information Overload

Decisions require clarity, not clutter.

- **Identify key metrics:** Focus on facts, KPIs, and data directly relevant to the decision.
- **Discard unnecessary details:** Too much information slows judgment and dilutes focus.
- **Use trusted sources:** Ensure accuracy and reliability rather than volume.

Targeted data collection sharpens insights and reduces decision fatigue.

Dose 5: Set Decision Deadlines — Commit to Timely Action

Time-bound decisions maintain momentum.

- **Establish clear timelines:** Define when a decision must be made and communicate it to stakeholders.
- **Avoid perpetual deliberation:** Even partial decisions are better than indefinite inaction.
- **Review urgency and impact:** Adjust deadlines based on strategic importance and operational needs.

Deadlines prevent bottlenecks and signal decisiveness to teams and leadership.

Dose 6: Delegate Where Possible — Empower Teams for Operational Decisions

Strategic focus comes from selective involvement.

- **Empower team members:** Let them handle operational or procedural decisions within their authority.
- **Maintain oversight without micromanaging:** Provide guidance and review mechanisms, but avoid unnecessary control.
- **Focus on high-level choices:** Reserve your attention for strategic, high-impact, or complex decisions.

Delegation multiplies organizational agility while strengthening decision ownership across teams.

Dose 7: Act Confidently — Communicate Decisions Clearly

Execution depends on clarity and conviction.

- **Announce decisions transparently:** Ensure all stakeholders understand the choice, rationale, and next steps.
- **Provide action plans:** Outline responsibilities, timelines, and expected outcomes.
- **Exude confidence without arrogance:** Your composure inspires team trust and alignment.

Confident communication transforms decisions into effective action.

Dose 8: Learn and Adjust — Integrate Lessons from Outcomes

Every decision is a learning opportunity.

- **Review results objectively:** Identify what worked, what didn't, and why.
- **Document lessons:** Maintain a decision log capturing rationale, execution, and impact.
- **Refine frameworks:** Adapt processes, criteria, and analytical approaches for future decisions.

Continuous learning strengthens decision-making immunity for increasingly complex situations.

Dose 9: Balance Risk and Reward — Be Bold, Yet Calculated

Executives are measured by decisive, strategic choices.

- **Assess risk-reward ratios:** Understand potential benefits, downsides, and mitigation strategies.
- **Take calculated risks:** Avoid unnecessary hesitation; measured boldness often drives innovation and growth.
- **Align with strategic goals:** Risk should never be taken in isolation — it must support overarching objectives.

Balanced risk-taking demonstrates judgment, courage, and executive readiness.

Dose 10: Build a Decision Track Record — Showcase Leadership Readiness

Consistent, successful decisions reinforce credibility.

- **Document achievements:** Record decisions, rationale, outcomes, and measurable impact.
- **Share learnings selectively:** Highlight decision effectiveness in reviews, meetings, or mentoring sessions.

- **Use the record for growth:** A proven track record signals readiness for higher responsibility and executive roles.

A strong decision history positions you as a leader who delivers results consistently.

Final Booster Dose : The Decision-Maker's Pledge

"I will focus on outcomes, prioritize strategically, and limit options to make timely, informed choices.

I will gather essential data, delegate operational decisions, act confidently, and learn from each result.

I will balance risk with reward and maintain a documented decision track record.

Through disciplined, thoughtful, and courageous decision-making, I will drive impact, inspire teams, and demonstrate readiness for executive leadership."

Executives are made, not born, through decisive action.

The Decision-Making Vaccine protects managers from hesitation, equips them to handle ambiguity, and builds credibility for higher roles.

Those who master timely, informed decision-making gain trust, visibility, and momentum toward executive leadership.

CHAPTER 24

EMPATHY VACCINE – PREVENTS ROBOTIC LEADERSHIP; STRENGTHENS TEAM LOYALTY.

Because emotional connection drives engagement, retention, and influence at higher leadership levels.

This vaccine strengthens your **ability to understand, connect, and inspire teams**, creating loyalty, trust, and sustainable high performance — key traits for executives.

The **Empathy Vaccine** is essential for managers aspiring to executive roles because **leaders who understand and connect with people inspire loyalty, engagement, and high performance.**

Here's a **story** first, followed by **Prescription**.

Story: "Ritika and the Empathy Vaccine"-From Task-*Focused Manager to Trusted Leader*

Ritika was a senior operations manager at a global logistics firm. She was excellent at meeting deadlines and driving performance, but her team often felt stressed and undervalued. Employee engagement surveys showed that while results were good, morale was low.

During a leadership coaching session, her mentor told her:

"Ritika, executive leaders don't just manage tasks; they manage people. Understanding your team's needs and perspectives is as important as hitting targets."

Determined to improve, Ritika decided to take her **Empathy Vaccine**.

Steps she implemented:

1. **Active Listening:** She scheduled one-on-one conversations with her team to understand challenges, aspirations, and concerns.
2. **Acknowledge Emotions:** She recognized achievements, frustrations, and workload pressures openly.
3. **Personalized Support:** She adjusted responsibilities and offered mentorship based on individual strengths and growth goals.
4. **Encourage Feedback:** She created safe channels for team members to share ideas and concerns without fear of judgment.
5. **Lead by Example:** Ritika demonstrated patience, understanding, and respect in all interactions.

Over time, her team became more engaged, collaborative, and proactive. Employees felt heard, and productivity improved. Leadership noticed the change, and Ritika was entrusted with leading a large cross-functional initiative. Within two years, her blend of results-oriented and empathetic leadership earned her a promotion to director, and she was considered for executive roles.

Reflecting on her journey, Ritika said:

"Empathy doesn't make you soft; it makes you strong. When people feel understood, they perform beyond expectations."

Prescription for Corporate Managers to Build the Empathy Vaccine

Empathy is **the cornerstone of effective leadership**. It is the ability to understand, connect with, and respond thoughtfully to the emotions, motivations, and challenges of your team and stakeholders. The **Empathy Vaccine** equips managers to strengthen relationships, foster trust, and build emotionally resilient teams. Below is a **10-Dose Prescription** to systematically cultivate empathy as a core leadership competency.

Dose 1: Listen Actively — Engage Fully, Not Partially

True empathy begins with listening.

- **Give undivided attention:** Maintain eye contact, minimize distractions, and focus completely on the speaker.
- **Ask clarifying questions:** Seek to understand emotions, reasoning, and context.

- **Observe non-verbal cues:** Tone, gestures, and facial expressions provide deeper insight than words alone.

Active listening ensures you grasp both the explicit and implicit needs of your team.

Dose 2: Acknowledge and Validate — Recognize Experiences Authentically

Validation fosters trust and psychological safety.

- **Celebrate achievements:** Publicly and privately acknowledge milestones and successes.
- **Recognize challenges:** Show understanding for frustrations or setbacks without judgment.
- **Use affirming language:** Phrases like "I see your effort" or "I understand why this is difficult" strengthen rapport.

Acknowledgment reassures team members that their contributions and feelings matter.

Dose 3: Personalize Support — Tailor Guidance and Recognition

Empathy requires customization.

- **Assign tasks thoughtfully:** Match responsibilities to individual strengths, aspirations, and development goals.
- **Provide targeted coaching:** Offer mentorship and resources suited to each team member's learning style.
- **Recognize personally:** Adjust praise and rewards to what motivates each individual — not a one-size-fits-all approach.

Personalized support nurtures engagement, growth, and loyalty.

Dose 4: Encourage Open Communication — Create Safe Channels

Open dialogue strengthens emotional immunity.

- **Foster trust:** Promote an environment where concerns, ideas, and mistakes can be shared without fear.
- **Solicit feedback regularly:** Ask team members for their perspectives on processes, leadership, and culture.
- **Respond constructively:** Validate input and act on feasible suggestions.

Safe communication spaces empower teams to be candid, innovative, and aligned.

Dose 5: Model Empathetic Behavior — Lead by Example

Empathy is contagious.

- **Demonstrate patience:** Respond calmly under stress and maintain composure during conflicts.
- **Show respect:** Treat all team members, peers, and stakeholders with dignity.
- **Be approachable:** Make yourself available for informal conversations and support.

Your behavior sets the cultural tone; empathy modeled at the top cascades throughout the team.

Dose 6: Balance Accountability and Compassion — Enforce Standards with Understanding

Empathy does not mean leniency.

- **Set clear expectations:** Ensure the team knows goals, deadlines, and quality standards.
- **Support through challenges:** Provide guidance, resources, and encouragement when performance issues arise.
- **Correct gently:** Address underperformance with constructive feedback rather than blame.

Balancing accountability and compassion maintains productivity while sustaining morale.

Dose 7: Understand Motivations — Decode Individual Drivers

People perform when their motivations are acknowledged.

- **Identify what drives each member:** Career growth, recognition, learning, purpose, or work-life balance.
- **Align tasks accordingly:** Assign responsibilities that resonate with intrinsic motivators.
- **Celebrate unique contributions:** Recognize achievements in ways that are meaningful to each person.

Understanding motivations enhances engagement, retention, and discretionary effort.

Dose 8: Resolve Conflicts Fairly — Mediate with Understanding

Conflict is inevitable; empathy guides resolution.

- **Listen to all perspectives:** Understand each party's concerns and underlying emotions.
- **Focus on solutions:** Address the issue constructively rather than assigning blame.

- **Maintain impartiality:** Ensure fairness and transparency in conflict resolution.

Empathetic conflict management builds trust and prevents long-term resentment.

Dose 9: Celebrate People, Not Just Results — Prioritize Human Wins

Recognition should honor effort, not only outcomes.

- **Acknowledge dedication and teamwork:** Highlight collaborative efforts, creative problem-solving, and persistence.
- **Public and private appreciation:** Adapt recognition based on individual preferences.
- **Connect achievements to purpose:** Reinforce how each contribution advances team and organizational goals.

Celebrating people fosters loyalty, motivation, and psychological safety.

Dose 10: Reflect and Adjust — Evolve with Feedback and Experience

Empathy is a continuous growth process.

- **Evaluate leadership style:** Regularly assess how your actions impact team morale, performance, and engagement.
- **Seek input:** Ask trusted team members for feedback on your approach.
- **Adapt proactively:** Modify communication, delegation, and support strategies based on insights.

Ongoing reflection strengthens emotional intelligence and long-term leadership effectiveness.

Final Booster: The Empathetic Leader's Pledge

"I will listen deeply, validate experiences, and tailor support to each individual.

I will encourage open communication, model empathy in every interaction, and balance accountability with compassion.

I will understand what motivates my team, resolve conflicts fairly, celebrate contributions, and continuously reflect to grow as an empathetic leader.

Through these actions, I will foster trust, engagement, and resilient teams capable of achieving sustainable excellence."

Executives are remembered for how they make people feel, not just the targets they hit.

The Empathy Vaccine transforms managers from task-driven supervisors into trusted, inspirational leaders.

Leaders who cultivate empathy gain loyalty, engagement, and influence — essential for promotion to executive levels.

CHAPTER 25

CRISIS-MANAGEMENT VACCINE – SHIELDS AGAINST PANIC IN TOUGH TIMES.

Because executives are chosen for composure, decisiveness, and guidance when the unexpected hits.

This vaccine strengthens your **ability to remain calm, analyze rapidly, and lead effectively during crises**, building credibility, trust, and readiness for executive roles.

The **Crisis-Management Vaccine** is essential for managers aspiring to executive roles because **leaders who remain calm, strategic, and decisive in crises earn trust, credibility, and long-term influence.**

Here's a **story** first, followed by **Prescription**.

Story: "Arjun and the Crisis-Management Vaccine"-*Leading Calmly When Everything's on Fire*

Arjun was a senior operations manager at a global manufacturing company. One quarter, a critical supply chain disruption threatened a major client delivery. Panic spread across the team, vendors, and even senior management.

Arjun noticed colleagues were overwhelmed, some making hasty decisions, and others freezing entirely. Instead of succumbing to stress, he decided to apply his **Crisis-Management Vaccine.**

Steps he implemented:

1. **Stay Calm and Assess:** He took a step back, gathered essential data, and prioritized the most critical issues.
2. **Communicate Transparently:** He updated the team and leadership with facts, not speculation, maintaining clarity and trust.
3. **Delegate Strategically:** He assigned tasks to the most capable team members, ensuring swift action without overloading anyone.
4. **Think in Contingencies:** Arjun developed short-term fixes while planning long-term preventive measures.
5. **Support and Motivate:** He encouraged the team, acknowledged stress, and celebrated small wins to maintain morale.

The results were remarkable. The client delivery was salvaged with minimal disruption, and the leadership team recognized Arjun for his composed, strategic, and effective handling of the crisis. Within months, he was promoted to director and considered for executive responsibilities because he had demonstrated **trustworthy leadership under pressure.**

Reflecting on his journey, Arjun said:

"Crises test leadership more than calm periods. The ability to think clearly and act decisively under pressure is what separates managers from executives."

Prescription for Corporate Managers to Build the Crisis-Management Vaccine

Crisis management is the lifeblood of organizational survival. It requires foresight, composure, and structured action under pressure. The Crisis-Management Vaccine is a metaphorical shield that equips corporate leaders to identify risks early, act decisively, and emerge stronger. Below is a 10-Dose Prescription to build lasting corporate immunity against uncertainty.

Dose 1: Awareness Injection — Detect Early, Act Swiftly

Crisis resilience begins with awareness.

- **Recognize early warning signs:** Monitor shifts in customer sentiment, employee morale, and market trends.
- **Establish data dashboards:** Track metrics that reveal brewing issues before they escalate.
- **Encourage open reporting:** Create a safe space for employees to flag red flags.

Early detection minimizes impact and builds organizational vigilance.

Dose 2: Agility Booster — Respond Fast, Adapt Faster

Agility transforms panic into progress.

- **Empower quick decision-making:** Delegate authority for rapid responses.
- **Encourage adaptability:** Train teams to pivot strategies without losing direction.
- **Document learnings:** Use every shift as a blueprint for future resilience.

An agile culture becomes the organization's reflex against volatility.

Dose 3: Communication Serum — Speak Clearly, Calmly, Consistently

In crisis, communication defines confidence.

- **Be transparent:** Share facts, not speculation.
- **Maintain frequency:** Silence breeds fear—regular updates build stability.
- **Use empathy in tone:** Combine honesty with assurance.

Clarity of message is the strongest antidote to confusion.

Dose 4: Empathy Infusion — Lead with Heart, Not Just Head

Empathy builds emotional immunity within teams.

- **Acknowledge stress:** Recognize the human toll of uncertainty.
- **Offer support:** Provide resources for mental and emotional well-being.
- **Foster connection:** Encourage dialogue, not directives.

Empathetic leadership sustains morale when logic alone cannot.

Dose 5: Strategy Stabilizer — Prepare, Don't Just React

Preparation transforms chaos into control.

- **Create crisis playbooks:** Define roles, responses, and escalation procedures.
- **Simulate scenarios:** Conduct drills to test readiness.
- **Evaluate outcomes:** Adjust strategies based on real-world insights.

Strategic foresight ensures calm amid turbulence.

Dose 6: Innovation Capsule — Experiment, Evolve, Excel

Innovation is the organization's vitamin for recovery.

- **Encourage creative thinking:** Crisis often sparks breakthrough ideas.
- **Pilot new methods:** Try small-scale experiments before large rollouts.
- **Reward boldness:** Recognize teams who take smart risks.

Innovation transforms adversity into opportunity.

Dose 7: Resilience Supplement — Bounce Back, Bounce Higher

Resilience is the endurance muscle of leadership.

- **Normalize setbacks:** Treat failure as a step toward improvement.
- **Build coping systems:** Offer coaching and mentoring during tough times.
- **Celebrate recovery stories:** Reinforce examples of perseverance.

Resilience ensures continuity when conditions collapse.

Dose 8: Collaboration Compound — Unite Strengths, Share Shields

Crisis immunity is collective, not individual.

- **Promote interdepartmental synergy:** Merge expertise from diverse domains.
- **Foster trust networks:** Build relationships that transcend hierarchies.
- **Share accountability:** Distribute responsibilities across teams.

Collaboration multiplies strength while dividing stress.

Dose 9: Integrity Serum — Choose Ethics Over Expediency

Integrity protects reputation when scrutiny is highest.

- **Adhere to values:** Let ethics guide every crisis decision.
- **Be accountable:** Admit mistakes and correct them openly.
- **Model transparency:** Lead by example, not by command.

Integrity earns lasting stakeholder trust—your organization's moral immunity.

Dose 10: Learning Booster — Reflect, Reinforce, Renew

Post-crisis reflection strengthens future response.

- **Conduct after-action reviews:** Document lessons and best practices.
- **Embed learnings:** Update systems, processes, and policies.
- **Celebrate growth:** Recognize improvement as progress.

Continuous learning ensures every crisis becomes a catalyst for evolution.

Final Booster Dose:

Vaccines work through repetition and reinforcement—and so does leadership resilience.

Revisit these 10 doses regularly to keep your organization mentally, morally, and strategically immunized against the next wave of uncertainty.

Executives aren't measured by calm periods but by how they steer through storms.

The Crisis-Management Vaccine equips managers to act decisively, guide teams under pressure, and emerge stronger, building credibility essential for executive promotion.

Leaders who thrive in crises inspire trust, loyalty, and long-term influence.

CHAPTER 26

INFLUENCE VACCINE – PROTECTS AGAINST IRRELEVANCE; ENSURES PEOPLE LISTEN.

Because even the best ideas fail if no one pays attention or acts on them.

This vaccine strengthens your **ability to communicate persuasively, build credibility, and gain buy-in**, ensuring your contributions drive action and position you for executive growth.

The **Influence Vaccine** is critical for managers aiming for executive roles because **executives succeed not just by doing great work, but by ensuring others notice, respect, and follow their ideas.**

Here's a **story** first, followed by **Prescription**.

Story: "Siddharth and the Influence Vaccine"-*From Doing Work to Driving Impact*

Siddharth was a senior marketing manager at a multinational firm. He consistently delivered high-quality campaigns and exceeded KPIs. However, during leadership discussions, he realized that his ideas were often overlooked, and strategic decisions went in favor of more vocal colleagues.

Recognizing the gap, Siddharth decided to take his **Influence Vaccine.**

Steps he implemented:

1. **Understand Stakeholders:** He mapped key decision-makers, their priorities, and pain points.
2. **Communicate with Impact:** He structured proposals around outcomes and benefits, not just tasks.
3. **Build Credibility:** He demonstrated expertise by consistently delivering results and sharing insights backed by data.
4. **Leverage Networks:** He cultivated relationships across teams to amplify his voice and gain allies.
5. **Listen and Adapt:** He adjusted his approach based on feedback and aligned his messaging to resonate with his audience.

Within a year, Siddharth's proposals started gaining traction. Leadership sought his input on strategic campaigns, and he became a go-to influencer for cross-functional initiatives. His enhanced visibility and persuasive ability accelerated his promotion to director and positioned him as a candidate for executive leadership.

Reflecting on his journey, Siddharth said:

"Influence isn't about being loud; it's about being heard, trusted, and respected. That's how you turn ideas into impact."

Prescription for Corporate Managers to Build the Influence Vaccine

Influence is the lifeblood of corporate leadership. It is not about authority, but about inspiring alignment, earning trust, and guiding action across diverse teams and hierarchies. The **Influence Vaccine** equips managers to build credibility, foster collaboration, and drive change without coercion. Below is a **10-Dose Prescription** to systematically cultivate influence as a powerful leadership competency.

Dose 1: Audience Awareness Injection — Know Whom You're Leading

True influence begins with understanding others.

- **Study motivations and priorities:** Identify what drives your stakeholders—goals, fears, and success metrics.
- **Recognize organizational culture:** Adapt your communication to align with the company's tone, values, and rhythm.
- **Map key influencers:** Know who shapes decisions formally and informally.

Influence grows when you speak to people's needs, not just your own agenda.

Dose 2: Outcome Orientation Booster — Speak in Impact, Not Activity

Leaders gain attention when they focus on results, not routines.

- **Frame discussions around outcomes:** Replace "what we did" with "what we achieved."
- **Quantify impact:** Highlight measurable ROI, cost savings, or performance gains.
- **Translate technical details into value:** Show how actions tie to strategic goals.

This dose ensures your ideas resonate with decision-makers who think in terms of results.

Dose 3: Credibility Serum — Demonstrate Expertise with Substance

Expertise is the immune system of influence—it protects your ideas from doubt.

- **Back claims with evidence:** Use data, reports, and benchmarks to support recommendations.
- **Share lessons from success and failure:** Both build authenticity.
- **Stay informed:** Regularly update yourself on industry and organizational trends.

Credibility transforms opinions into trusted guidance.

Dose 4: Alliance Builder Capsule — Multiply Strength Through Networks

Influence thrives through connection.

- **Cultivate relationships across departments:** Don't limit influence to your direct circle.
- **Collaborate on cross-functional projects:** Build allies through shared success.
- **Acknowledge others publicly:** Recognition creates goodwill and loyalty.

A well-connected leader spreads ideas faster and gains wider support.

Dose 5: Consistency Stabilizer — Build Trust Brick by Brick

Trust is the strongest stabilizer of influence.

- **Deliver on promises:** Reliability strengthens your professional brand.
- **Stay aligned with values:** Let integrity guide decisions even under pressure.
- **Communicate regularly:** Predictable communication builds comfort and faith.

Consistency turns influence from a temporary effect into a lasting trait.

Dose 6: Listening Tonic — Influence Begins with Understanding

The power to persuade comes from the ability to listen.

- **Ask open-ended questions:** Encourage others to share their perspectives freely.
- **Reflect understanding:** Paraphrase or summarize key points to show engagement.

- **Adapt your message:** Align communication to their needs, not your script.

Listening transforms influence from persuasion to partnership.

Dose 7: Confidence-with-Humility Infusion — Lead Boldly, Learn Bravely

Confidence earns attention; humility earns respect.

- **Present with authority:** Express ideas with conviction and clarity.
- **Stay open to feedback:** Invite diverse viewpoints without defensiveness.
- **Admit limits:** Acknowledge when you need input or expertise from others.

Balanced leaders inspire trust because they combine strength with self-awareness.

Dose 8: Storytelling Syrup — Make Your Message Stick

Facts inform, but stories inspire.

- **Use relatable examples:** Bring data to life through human stories or case studies.
- **Highlight transformation:** Show how challenges evolved into success.
- **Craft emotional connection:** People remember how you made them feel.

Storytelling anchors your influence in memory and meaning.

Dose 9: Visibility Booster — Be Seen, Be Heard, Be Valued

Unseen contributions seldom inspire.

- **Share accomplishments strategically:** Highlight outcomes in reports and presentations.
- **Speak up in forums:** Use meetings to position ideas that advance collective goals.
- **Maintain a professional presence:** Leverage internal communications or digital platforms to showcase expertise.

Visibility ensures your influence reaches beyond your immediate team.

Dose 10: Mentorship Injection — Multiply Influence Through Others

Influence deepens when it uplifts others.

- **Coach emerging talent:** Invest time in guiding colleagues to success.
- **Create learning spaces:** Share insights, frameworks, and feedback generously.
- **Model growth mindset:** Show that leadership is about collective elevation.

Mentorship is the booster shot that transforms individual influence into organizational legacy.

Final booster Dose:

Influence cannot be injected overnight—it must be built dose by dose through credibility, consistency, and care. Administer these 10 doses regularly, and you'll develop the leadership immunity required to navigate complex corporate ecosystems with authority and authenticity.

Executives are remembered for the impact they create and the people they inspire, not just the tasks they complete.

The Influence Vaccine ensures your ideas are heard, respected, and acted upon.

Managers who cultivate influence accelerate promotions, expand their impact, and secure credibility essential for executive leadership.

CHAPTER 27

CULTURAL-SENSITIVITY VACCINE – IMMUNITY FOR WORKING WITH DIVERSE TEAMS GLOBALLY.

Because executive success in global organizations depends on understanding, respecting, and leveraging diversity.

This vaccine strengthens your **ability to navigate cultural nuances, build inclusive teams, and lead effectively across geographies**, essential for executive credibility and global impact.

The **Cultural-Sensitivity Vaccine** is essential for managers aiming for executive roles because **leaders who understand, respect, and adapt to diverse cultures foster collaboration, avoid conflicts, and gain credibility in global organizations.**

Here's a **story** first, followed by **Prescription**.

Story: "Leena and the Cultural-Sensitivity Vaccine"- *Thriving Across Borders and Cultures*

Leena was a regional operations manager at a global tech company. Her team included members from India, Germany, Brazil, and Japan. While she excelled at managing local tasks, cross-cultural misunderstandings sometimes led to delays, miscommunications, and frustration.

During a leadership program, her mentor told her:

"Leena, executive leaders don't just manage teams—they lead people across cultures. Sensitivity to values, communication styles, and work norms is critical for global impact."

Determined to improve, Leena decided to take her **Cultural-Sensitivity Vaccine**.

Steps she implemented:

1. **Learn Cultural Norms:** She studied her team members' backgrounds, holidays, communication styles, and decision-making preferences.
2. **Adapt Communication:** She adjusted emails, meetings, and feedback approaches to respect cultural differences.
3. **Foster Inclusion:** She encouraged all team members to voice opinions, valuing diverse perspectives.
4. **Resolve Misunderstandings Diplomatically:** She mediated conflicts by understanding root causes linked to cultural perspectives.

5. **Celebrate Diversity:** She acknowledged cultural festivals, created inclusive rituals, and promoted awareness in team meetings.

Over time, team cohesion improved dramatically. Collaboration across regions became seamless, productivity increased, and senior leadership noticed Leena's ability to manage a truly global team. Within 18 months, she was promoted to director of international operations and positioned for an executive role overseeing multiple regions.

Reflecting on her journey, Leena said:

"Cultural sensitivity isn't optional—it's strategic. Respect and understanding create loyalty, collaboration, and results across borders."

Prescription for Corporate Managers to Build the Cultural-Sensitivity Vaccine

Cultural sensitivity is no longer optional—it is a leadership imperative in today's globalized corporate landscape. It enables managers to collaborate seamlessly across borders, respect differences, and turn diversity into organizational strength. The **Cultural-Sensitivity Vaccine** helps leaders build mutual respect, trust, and inclusion across varied backgrounds. Below is a **10-Dose Prescription** to cultivate cultural intelligence as a core leadership vaccine for success in a global workplace.

Dose 1: Cultural Awareness Injection — Learn, Observe, and Respect

True inclusion begins with understanding.

- **Study team members' backgrounds:** Learn about work norms, traditions, and communication patterns.
- **Respect cultural practices:** Acknowledge holidays, observances, and values that shape behavior.
- **Observe interactions:** Notice subtle cues—what is considered polite, assertive, or respectful may differ across cultures.

Awareness is the foundation of sensitivity—it transforms ignorance into understanding.

Dose 2: Communication Adaptability Serum — Speak with Context, Not Assumption

One size never fits all in communication.

- **Adjust your tone and language:** Balance directness, formality, and emotional expressiveness to suit each culture.
- **Be mindful of non-verbal cues:** Gestures, pauses, and eye contact vary in meaning globally.
- **Clarify with empathy:** Encourage questions to ensure mutual understanding without judgment.

Adapted communication eliminates friction and builds cross-cultural trust.

Dose 3: Inclusion Booster — Invite, Involve, and Integrate

Inclusion is not passive—it's intentional.

- **Create equal opportunities to speak:** Actively invite quieter or less represented voices.
- **Value diverse perspectives:** Make cultural diversity an asset in problem-solving and creativity.
- **Encourage shared leadership:** Let team members from different regions or backgrounds lead projects.

Inclusion transforms cultural variety into collective brilliance.

Dose 4: Diplomacy Capsule — Resolve with Sensitivity, Not Authority

Conflict is natural; insensitivity is not.

- **Identify cultural triggers:** Understand if disagreements stem from communication style, hierarchy, or values.
- **Mediate with neutrality:** Focus on understanding before judging.
- **Preserve dignity for all:** Ensure outcomes honor all parties' perspectives.

Diplomatic conflict resolution turns tension into trust.

Dose 5: Relationship-Building Tonic — Connect Beyond Borders

Influence expands through genuine cross-cultural relationships.

- **Network globally:** Engage with peers and clients from different regions to understand their worldviews.
- **Show genuine curiosity:** Ask about traditions, cuisines, or customs in professional interactions.
- **Maintain regular touchpoints:** Respect time zones and cultural etiquette in follow-ups.

Relationships built on respect create bridges that strategy alone cannot.

Dose 6: Awareness Promoter — Celebrate Diversity, Cultivate Unity

Awareness fosters appreciation.

- **Organize cultural learning sessions:** Encourage employees to share insights from their cultures.
- **Celebrate international milestones:** Recognize events like World Culture Day or regional festivals.
- **Highlight diversity stories:** Showcase how different perspectives drive success.

Awareness initiatives make diversity visible, valued, and vibrant.

Dose 7: Open-Mindedness Infusion — Replace Judgment with Curiosity

Cultural intelligence grows from humility.

- **Challenge stereotypes:** Question preconceived notions about nationalities, accents, or behaviors.
- **Be willing to unlearn:** Replace outdated assumptions with informed understanding.
- **Learn from discomfort:** Growth happens when perspectives collide respectfully.

Open-mindedness transforms diversity into dialogue, not division.

Dose 8: Leadership-by-Example Serum — Model Respect and Flexibility

Cultural sensitivity begins at the top.

- **Demonstrate respect consistently:** Be punctual for global meetings, use inclusive language, and acknowledge every voice.
- **Adapt leadership style:** Shift between collaborative, consultative, or directive approaches depending on cultural context.
- **Show curiosity publicly:** Ask questions about others' experiences without bias or judgment.

When leaders model sensitivity, teams mirror inclusion.

Dose 9: Diversity Utilization Supplement — Harness Collective Strengths

Cultural diversity is a performance enhancer when leveraged well.

- **Assign roles by strengths:** Recognize how cultural work styles—individualistic or collective—impact efficiency.
- **Encourage knowledge sharing:** Let teams learn from each other's unique approaches.
- **Integrate global insights:** Apply multicultural perspectives to innovation, marketing, and problem-solving.

Leveraging diversity transforms difference into competitive advantage.

Dose 10: Lifelong Learning Booster — Grow Through Every Interaction

Cultural fluency is a journey, not a destination.

- **Stay curious:** Treat every cross-cultural exchange as a learning opportunity.
- **Seek feedback:** Ask how your communication or leadership style is perceived in different cultures.
- **Update continuously:** Read, travel, and engage in global experiences.

Learning ensures your cultural sensitivity remains dynamic, not static.

Final Booster Dose:

Cultural sensitivity is the ultimate vaccine against misunderstanding and exclusion. Administer these 10 doses regularly—through awareness, adaptability, and appreciation—and you will cultivate a globally fluent mindset that thrives in every boardroom, culture, and country.

Executives are judged not just by results, but by their ability to unite and lead diverse teams.

The Cultural-Sensitivity Vaccine ensures managers thrive in global environments, build trust across cultures, and position themselves for executive leadership.

Leaders who master cultural sensitivity gain influence, loyalty, and career immunity in a global corporate world.

CHAPTER 28

VISION VACCINE – PREVENTS SHORT-SIGHTEDNESS; INSPIRES OTHERS WITH CLARITY.

Because executives aren't just problem-solvers — they're pathfinders who guide teams toward meaningful long-term outcomes.

This vaccine strengthens your **ability to think strategically, articulate a compelling future, and rally others around it**, building credibility and influence essential for executive leadership.

The **Vision Vaccine** is crucial for managers aiming for executive roles because **leaders who think long-term, articulate a compelling future, and inspire teams are positioned for strategic influence and career growth.**

Here's a **story** first, followed by **Prescription.**

Story: "Ananya and the Vision Vaccine"-*Leading with Eyes on the Horizon*

Ananya was a senior product manager at a tech company. She excelled at executing projects, meeting deadlines, and optimizing processes. Yet, she noticed that while her team was efficient, they often lacked motivation, direction, and a sense of purpose beyond immediate tasks.

During a leadership workshop, her mentor challenged her:

"Ananya, managers execute plans; executives create them. You need to inspire your team with a clear vision for where you're going and why it matters."

Determined to grow, Ananya decided to take her **Vision Vaccine**.

Steps she implemented:

1. **Define Long-Term Goals:** She mapped a roadmap for product development aligned with company strategy and market trends.
2. **Articulate the Vision Clearly:** She communicated how each team member's work contributed to the bigger picture.
3. **Engage the Team:** She held brainstorming sessions, encouraged innovation, and linked day-to-day tasks to strategic outcomes.
4. **Monitor Progress Strategically:** She tracked milestones and celebrated achievements, reinforcing alignment with the vision.
5. **Adjust with Agility:** She adapted the vision as market dynamics shifted but kept the overarching purpose intact.

The results were transformative. Team members felt motivated, ownership increased, and innovation improved. Leadership recognized Ananya's ability to see beyond tasks and inspire strategic thinking. Within a year, she was promoted to director and later positioned for an executive role overseeing multiple product lines.

Reflecting on her journey, Ananya said:

"Vision isn't just about predicting the future; it's about creating a path that motivates people to follow you willingly."

Prescription for Corporate Managers to Build the Vision Vaccine

Just as a vaccine strengthens immunity against uncertainty, this *Vision Vaccine* fortifies corporate leaders against short-term distractions and strategic drift. Administer each "dose" consistently for sustained visionary leadership.

Dose 1: Think Long-Term

Strengthen your strategic foresight by focusing on outcomes that extend beyond quarterly goals.

Anticipate future trends, emerging technologies, and industry shifts. Train your mind to look 3, 5, or even 10 years ahead — envisioning how today's actions build tomorrow's success.

Dose 2: Create a Clear Vision

Articulate a destination that your team can see, feel, and believe in.

A powerful vision is not just a statement — it's a shared purpose that connects every member to a larger goal. Define what success looks like and why it matters.

Dose 3: Communicate Purposefully

Translate the big picture into daily meaning.

Link every project, meeting, and milestone to the overarching purpose. When team members understand *why* their work matters, they act with greater ownership and enthusiasm.

Dose 4: Engage the Team

Make vision-building a collaborative exercise.

Invite diverse perspectives, ideas, and innovations from across the team. When employees participate in shaping the path forward, they become active partners in realizing the vision.

Dose 5: Monitor and Adapt

A true visionary tracks progress with flexibility.

Review milestones regularly, assess outcomes, and be willing to pivot when necessary — without losing sight of the long-term destination. Adaptability keeps your vision relevant and resilient.

Dose 6: Lead by Example

Be the embodiment of the vision you preach.

Show consistency in your actions, priorities, and decisions. When your team sees you making choices aligned with the long-term goal, they follow with conviction and trust.

Dose 7: Foster Strategic Thinking

Encourage your team to look beyond immediate deliverables.

Ask them: "How does this task contribute to our larger objective?" Help them connect the dots between their roles and the organization's broader strategy — cultivating strategic thinkers, not just executors.

Dose 8: Celebrate Milestones

Acknowledge and reward progress along the journey.

Each small victory strengthens belief in the vision. Recognizing contributions publicly sustains motivation and reinforces the shared sense of achievement.

Dose 9: Inspire Confidence

Your conviction is contagious.

Communicate with clarity and confidence — even during uncertainty. When you show unwavering belief in the vision, others draw courage and stability from your leadership.

Dose 10: Align with Organizational Goals

Ensure your vision is in harmony with the company's mission and strategy.

Alignment demonstrates maturity, readiness for executive roles, and the ability to balance ambition with organizational direction. A vision that supports the larger purpose creates collective momentum.

Recommended Dosage:

Take one "dose" daily in thought and action. Reassess quarterly. Repeat indefinitely for sustained leadership vitality.

Executives are defined not just by what they do, but by where they lead others.

The Vision Vaccine ensures managers avoid short-term thinking, inspire teams with clarity, and position themselves as strategic leaders.

Leaders who cultivate vision create alignment, engagement, and career immunity in the path to executive roles.

CHAPTER 29

ETHICS VACCINE – PROTECTS REPUTATION; IMMUNITY AGAINST CORRUPTION TRAPS.

Because executives are chosen for reliability, integrity, and trustworthiness, not just performance.

This vaccine strengthens your **ability to make principled decisions, maintain transparency, and uphold credibility**, which protects your career and reputation while positioning you for executive leadership.

The **Ethics Vaccine** is critical for managers aiming for executive roles because **leaders with integrity build trust, credibility, and long-term influence — essential qualities for sustainable career growth.**

Here's a **story** first, followed by **Prescription**.

Story: "Rohit and the Ethics Vaccine"-Integrity as the Foundation of Leadership

Rohit was a senior finance manager at a multinational corporation. Early in his career, he faced subtle pressure to bend accounting rules to present a rosier financial picture to leadership. While it seemed "small" at the time, he knew it could jeopardize his reputation and the company's integrity.

Instead of taking shortcuts, Rohit decided to take his **Ethics Vaccine**.

Steps he implemented:

1. **Follow Rules Rigorously:** He ensured all financial reports were accurate, transparent, and compliant with laws and internal policies.
2. **Speak Up:** He raised concerns about questionable practices, providing constructive alternatives.
3. **Model Integrity:** He demonstrated honesty in all dealings with clients, vendors, and colleagues.
4. **Encourage Ethical Practices:** He mentored juniors to prioritize ethics over shortcuts.
5. **Document and Protect:** He maintained proper records to defend decisions and uphold accountability.

The outcome was transformative. Rohit became known as a trustworthy, principled manager. Leadership valued his reliability, and his ethical stance earned him respect across departments. When a major corporate restructuring occurred, he was promoted to director and later considered for an executive role because his integrity had established him as a leader who could be trusted with critical decisions.

Reflecting on his journey, Rohit said:

"Ethics isn't about avoiding mistakes; it's about creating a reputation that people can trust. That trust opens doors that talent alone cannot."

Prescription for Corporate Managers to Build the Ethics Vaccine

Just as vaccines protect the body from infection, the *Ethics Vaccine* immunizes corporate leaders against moral compromise, reputational risk, and decision-making under pressure.

Each dose builds a stronger ethical core — ensuring that integrity becomes second nature, not situational.

Dose 1: Adhere to Rules and Policies

The first line of ethical defense is compliance.

Familiarize yourself with laws, regulations, and your company's code of conduct. Follow Standard Operating Procedures (SOPs) diligently, even when no one is watching.

A disciplined adherence to policies signals professionalism and safeguards the organization from legal and reputational harm.

Take daily — compliance builds credibility faster than charisma.

Dose 2: Be Transparent

Transparency is the oxygen of ethical leadership.

Communicate decisions, processes, and results openly with your stakeholders — whether peers, subordinates, or clients. Clarity breeds trust, while secrecy breeds suspicion.

Invite scrutiny of your actions and demonstrate that your motives are aligned with fairness and accountability.

Take whenever communication occurs — transparency keeps ethics alive.

Dose 3: Raise Concerns Constructively

When you see something wrong, don't stay silent.

Address unethical practices tactfully — focusing on facts, not blame. Present constructive alternatives or corrective measures.

Being the voice of conscience in the room takes courage, but it also earns respect and sets a precedent for moral courage across the organization.

Take when integrity is tested — courage is your immune booster.

Dose 4: Lead by Example

Your conduct defines the culture around you.

Demonstrate honesty, fairness, and respect in every interaction — especially under pressure. When you walk the talk, your team follows your lead naturally.

Ethics, when modeled consistently, becomes a silent yet powerful form of leadership.

Take continuously — your example is your most persuasive ethical argument.

Dose 5: Mentor on Ethics

Share your ethical compass with others.

Coach your juniors and peers to uphold principled behavior even in difficult situations. Discuss real-world ethical dilemmas and guide them on responsible decision-making.

Creating a chain of ethical influence ensures sustainability of values beyond your personal sphere.

Administer weekly — mentorship multiplies moral immunity.

Dose 6: Document Decisions

Transparency thrives on traceability.

Keep clear records of decisions, approvals, and rationales — especially in sensitive or high-stakes matters. Documentation not only ensures accountability but also protects you and your team in case of disputes or audits.

An ethical paper trail is a sign of both prudence and integrity.

Take before every key decision — recordkeeping prevents ethical erosion.

Dose 7: Avoid Shortcuts

Reject the temptation of quick wins that compromise long-term credibility.

Shortcuts often lead to setbacks disguised as success. Choose diligence over speed, and principle over convenience.

Ethical success may take longer, but it endures far beyond fleeting rewards.

Take when pressured — integrity is the best antidote to expedience.

Dose 8: Cultivate a Culture of Trust

Build an environment where honesty is valued and misconduct has no place to hide.

Recognize and reward ethical choices as visibly as performance milestones. Encourage open conversations about moral challenges.

Trust grows when people feel safe to do what's right — not just what's easy.

Take with every interaction — trust is the daily vitamin of ethical culture.

Dose 9: Evaluate Long-Term Impact

Think beyond immediate gains.

Before making decisions, ask: "Will this action protect our reputation and relationships in the long run?"

Ethical leaders prioritize sustainability, fairness, and reputation over temporary advantages.

Take before every major action — foresight prevents ethical fatigue.

Dose 10: Continuous Reflection

Ethical immunity requires regular introspection.

Periodically assess your decisions, motivations, and behaviors. Acknowledge missteps, learn from them, and recommit to doing better.

Ethical strength grows through humility, self-awareness, and the willingness to evolve.

Take at the end of every week — reflection renews your moral immunity.

Recommended Dosage:

Administer one ethical dose every day through thought, decision, and action.

For best results, combine with empathy, transparency, and accountability. Side effects may include enhanced credibility, deep respect, and an unshakable reputation.

Executives are remembered for the integrity of their decisions, not just the outcomes.

The Ethics Vaccine protects managers from short-term temptations, builds lasting trust, and positions them for executive leadership.

Leaders who cultivate ethics gain career immunity, influence, and respect — the true currency of sustainable corporate growth.

CHAPTER 30

NEGOTIATION VACCINE – IMMUNITY AGAINST UNFAIR DEALS & LOPSIDED CONTRACTS.

Because executives are judged on their ability to secure favorable outcomes without compromising trust or relationships.

This vaccine strengthens your **ability to prepare, negotiate, and achieve fair, strategic agreements**, ensuring organizational value, credibility, and executive readiness.

The **Negotiation Vaccine** is essential for managers aspiring to executive roles because **leaders who negotiate effectively protect organizational interests, secure resources, and create win-win outcomes, building credibility and influence.**

Here's a **story** first, followed by **Prescription**.

Story: "Karan and the Negotiation Vaccine"-T*urning Every Deal into a Win-Win*

Karan was a procurement manager at a multinational firm. He often noticed that his team would accept vendor terms without pushing for better pricing, deadlines, or quality guarantees. While deals were completed, the company sometimes lost margin or faced operational challenges.

Realizing the gap, Karan decided to take his **Negotiation Vaccine**.

Steps he implemented:

1. **Prepare Thoroughly:** He researched market rates, vendor performance, and alternative options before discussions.
2. **Define Objectives Clearly:** He identified must-haves, negotiable items, and fallback positions.
3. **Listen Actively:** He understood vendor constraints and motivations to find mutually beneficial solutions.
4. **Communicate Assertively:** He presented proposals confidently, backing requests with data and rationale.
5. **Aim for Win-Win:** He sought agreements that created value for both the company and vendors.

The outcome was remarkable. Karan successfully renegotiated several long-term contracts, saving the company significant costs while maintaining strong vendor relationships. Leadership noticed his strategic thinking and ability to protect the organization's interests. Within a year, Karan was promoted to senior manager, and later considered for executive-level roles overseeing global procurement.

Reflecting on his journey, Karan said:

"Negotiation isn't about winning every point—it's about ensuring fairness, protecting value, and building relationships that last. That's how executives secure results sustainably."

Prescription for Corporate Managers to Build the Negotiation Vaccine

Negotiation is not a battle to win — it's a bridge to build.

The *Negotiation Vaccine* equips managers with the emotional intelligence, analytical rigor, and strategic foresight to turn conflicting interests into collaborative outcomes. Each dose strengthens your ability to balance assertiveness with empathy, ensuring long-term value and trust in every deal.

Dose 1: Do Your Homework — Preparation Is Your First Shield

Effective negotiation begins long before you enter the room.

Research market benchmarks, industry standards, competitor practices, and alternative vendors. Study the contract details, historical dealings, and the other party's possible leverage points.

Preparation transforms uncertainty into confidence and positions you to anticipate counterarguments with precision.

Take before every meeting — informed negotiators never get cornered.

Dose 2: Set Clear Objectives — Define Your Battlefield and Boundaries

Go into every negotiation with clarity of purpose.

Identify your top priorities, acceptable compromises, and non-negotiable limits. Create fallback positions that still align with your organization's long-term interests.

When objectives are well-defined, emotions don't dictate outcomes — strategy does.

Take at the planning stage — clarity is the antidote to confusion.

Dose 3: Listen and Understand — Decode Before You Decide

True negotiation power lies in understanding the other side.

Listen actively to the motivations, constraints, and underlying interests of your counterpart. Ask open-ended questions to uncover what truly drives their position.

Empathy in negotiation builds bridges where aggression builds walls.

Take during every discussion — listening builds leverage.

Dose 4: Communicate Clearly — Words Are Your Most Potent Tool

State your case with confidence, clarity, and data-driven rationale.

Avoid vague language; instead, present facts, figures, and logical benefits. Use assertive but respectful communication that demonstrates professionalism and conviction.

A clear message reduces misunderstanding and enhances perceived credibility.

Take throughout the conversation — clarity vaccinates against misinterpretation.

Dose 5: Seek Win-Win Outcomes — Collaboration Over Confrontation

Negotiation should aim for partnership, not dominance.

Strive for agreements that add mutual value — where both parties feel respected and satisfied.

A win-win mindset fosters long-term alliances and repeat opportunities rather than one-time victories.

Take during conclusion — mutual gain strengthens immunity to conflict.

Dose 6: Stay Calm and Patient — Emotional Control Is Strategic Strength

Negotiations often test patience and composure.

Stay calm even under provocation or pressure. Avoid emotional reactions that cloud judgment or weaken your position.

Patience allows you to read situations clearly and make decisions grounded in logic, not ego.

Take under stress — calmness is the most effective antidote to impulsiveness.

Dose 7: Document Agreements — Lock the Understanding in Writing

Verbal agreements fade; written ones endure.

Ensure that all negotiated terms are accurately documented, reviewed for legal compliance, and communicated to relevant teams. Maintain version control and follow through with accountability measures.

Documentation not only prevents disputes but also protects organizational integrity.

Take immediately post-negotiation — documentation seals the deal ethically.

Dose 8: Leverage Relationships — Build Networks That Negotiate for You

Negotiation strength grows through reputation and rapport.

Invest in building trust with stakeholders, clients, and vendors over time.

A foundation of respect and reliability ensures smoother discussions, better concessions, and faster consensus.

Take daily — relationship capital is the most sustainable negotiation asset.

Dose 9: Know When to Walk Away — Protect Value Over Vanity

Not every deal deserves a signature.

Recognize when the terms pose unacceptable risks or fail to align with organizational goals. Walking away confidently preserves integrity, credibility, and future leverage.

A wise "no" today often opens doors for a stronger "yes" tomorrow.

Take when tempted by compromise — walking away is sometimes the strongest move.

Dose 10: Review and Learn — Build Immunity Through Reflection

Every negotiation leaves behind lessons.

Analyze what worked, what didn't, and where you could have communicated more effectively. Document insights to refine your approach for future engagements.

Continuous learning transforms negotiation from a skill into an instinct.

Take after every deal — reflection is your lifelong booster dose.

Recommended Dosage:

Administer one dose before, during, and after every negotiation cycle.

For best results, combine with empathy, preparation, and patience.

Side effects include increased confidence, stronger relationships, and consistent strategic wins.

Executives are recognized for their ability to create value while protecting the organization's interests.

The Negotiation Vaccine equips managers to secure fair, strategic deals, strengthen credibility, and gain influence essential for executive leadership.

Leaders who master negotiation combine strategic insight, assertiveness, and fairness — key ingredients for career immunity and growth.

CHAPTER 31

TECHNOLOGY VACCINE – STAY IMMUNE TO OBSOLESCENCE BY EMBRACING AI, DIGITAL TOOLS.

Because executives are valued for innovation, adaptability, and the ability to leverage technology for strategic advantage.

This vaccine strengthens your **ability to adopt new tools, harness digital insights, and drive innovation,** ensuring career relevance and positioning you for executive leadership.

The **Technology Vaccine** is critical for managers aspiring to executive roles because **leaders who embrace emerging technology and digital tools stay relevant, make informed decisions, and drive innovation in a rapidly evolving corporate world.**

Here's a **story** first, followed by **Prescription.**

Story: "Sneha and the Technology Vaccine"-*From Manual Processes to Digital Leadership*

Sneha was a mid-level operations manager at a global logistics company. While her team consistently met targets, she noticed inefficiencies in reporting, workflow management, and data analysis due to reliance on outdated tools. Her peers who adopted newer digital tools were recognized as more forward-thinking by leadership.

Determined to stay ahead, Sneha decided to take her **Technology Vaccine.**

Steps she implemented:

1. **Learn Emerging Tools:** She enrolled in courses on AI-driven analytics, workflow automation, and cloud collaboration platforms.
2. **Pilot Digital Solutions:** She implemented automated reporting, predictive analytics, and process optimization tools within her team.
3. **Upskill Her Team:** She trained team members to use new technologies, increasing efficiency and reducing errors.
4. **Integrate Data-Driven Decision Making:** She relied on insights from digital tools to make faster, more accurate decisions.
5. **Share Results:** She showcased measurable improvements to senior leadership, demonstrating innovation and impact.

The results were transformational. Sneha's team became more efficient, errors dropped, and decision-making became faster and more strategic. Leadership recognized her as a forward-thinking manager capable of scaling operations and leveraging technology to drive growth. Within a year, she was promoted to director and positioned for executive-level roles overseeing digital transformation initiatives.

Reflecting on her journey, Sneha said:

"Technology doesn't replace people — it amplifies impact. Staying current is no longer optional; it's how you future-proof your career."

Prescription for Corporate Managers to Build the Technology Vaccine

In today's digital-first economy, technology is not just an enabler — it is the bloodstream of organizational success.

The *Technology Vaccine* equips corporate managers with digital immunity against disruption, obsolescence, and inefficiency. Each dose builds resilience, adaptability, and foresight — ensuring that technology becomes a competitive advantage rather than a challenge.

Dose 1: Stay Updated on Trends — Build Awareness Before Adoption

The first step to technological resilience is awareness.

Monitor emerging trends in artificial intelligence, automation, data analytics, cybersecurity, and industry-specific digital tools. Subscribe to thought leadership journals, attend tech expos, and engage in professional networks.

Staying updated helps managers make informed decisions that anticipate change rather than react to it.

Take daily — awareness is your first defense against technological decay.

Dose 2: Invest in Learning — Upgrade Your Own Operating System

Technology evolves faster than experience alone can keep up.

Enroll in online courses, attend workshops, or pursue professional certifications to deepen your understanding of digital transformation. Learning must become a continuous process — not a one-time event.

Managers who learn proactively lead with credibility and confidence.

Take quarterly — continuous learning is the booster that keeps your skills future-ready.

Dose 3: Implement Digital Solutions — Turn Knowledge into Action

Digital transformation succeeds when strategy meets execution.

Identify repetitive, manual, or time-consuming workflows that can be automated or streamlined. Explore enterprise tools for project management, customer relations, data visualization, or collaboration.

Implementation bridges the gap between knowing technology and truly using it for impact.

Take as needed — digital adoption is the cure for operational inefficiency.

Dose 4: Upskill Your Team — Spread Immunity Across the Organization

A digitally enabled team is an empowered team.

Organize training sessions, internal demos, and hands-on workshops that build comfort with new tools. Encourage knowledge-sharing among team members to foster collective growth.

When every individual is confident with technology, the entire organization becomes agile and future-ready.

Take monthly — team upskilling multiplies your organization's digital immunity.

Dose 5: Leverage Data for Decisions — Turn Information into Intelligence

Data is the new vaccine against guesswork.

Utilize analytics dashboards, performance reports, and predictive tools to guide strategic choices. Move beyond intuition — let insights from real-time data shape planning, budgeting, and performance management.

Data-driven leadership enhances precision, accountability, and results.

Take before every major decision — data ensures accuracy and consistency.

Dose 6: Showcase Impact — Prove That Technology Works

Leaders must translate digital progress into tangible business outcomes.

Highlight improvements such as reduced turnaround times, increased revenue, improved customer satisfaction, or streamlined operations. Share success stories across teams and departments to inspire adoption.

Visibility of impact builds organizational confidence in digital transformation.

Take after each implementation — impact demonstration reinforces belief in innovation.

Dose 7: Experiment and Innovate — Adopt a Lab Mindset

Technology thrives in cultures that tolerate experimentation.

Pilot new tools, run controlled trials, collect feedback, and refine implementation before scaling. Treat failure as feedback — each experiment contributes to organizational learning.

Innovation without fear ensures continuous progress in a fast-changing landscape.

Take whenever possible — innovation is the booster shot of digital evolution.

Dose 8: Collaborate Across Functions — Break Silos, Build Systems

Digital success is collective, not isolated.

Collaborate with finance, operations, marketing, and HR to share learnings and align systems. Cross-functional teams enhance efficiency, reduce duplication, and ensure coherent adoption.

Shared digital intelligence strengthens organizational connectivity and agility.

Take collaboratively—digital transformation is a team immunization effort.

Dose 9: Prepare for Change — Build an Adaptive Mindset

Technology disruption is inevitable; resistance is optional.

Cultivate openness to change by viewing every technological shift as an opportunity to improve. Equip your team to manage transitions smoothly through transparent communication and structured training.

Adaptability ensures continuity even amidst rapid evolution.

Take during every transition — adaptability prevents resistance and fatigue.

Dose 10: Integrate Strategy with Technology — Align Tools with Purpose

Technology without strategy is noise.

Ensure that every digital investment supports organizational goals such as customer satisfaction, efficiency, profitability, or innovation. Integrate technology planning with business strategy reviews and performance dashboards.

When technology and vision align, transformation becomes sustainable and value-driven.

Take at leadership level — alignment is the final immunity against digital chaos.

Recommended Dosage:

Administer one dose per project cycle and reinforce quarterly with team-wide learning initiatives.

Combine with doses of innovation, adaptability, and communication for full-spectrum digital immunity.

Side effects include heightened efficiency, faster decision-making, and long-term relevance.

Executives are defined by their ability to innovate, adapt, and leverage technology strategically.

The Technology Vaccine ensures managers remain relevant, amplify impact, and secure career immunity in a digital corporate world.

Leaders who embrace technology drive efficiency, innovation, and influence — key traits for executive growth.

CHAPTER 32

WELLBEING VACCINE – BALANCE HEALTH, FAMILY, AND CAREER TO PREVENT BURNOUT.

Because executives who neglect wellbeing risk poor decisions, stress, and short-lived success.

This vaccine strengthens your **ability to maintain physical, mental, and emotional health while managing responsibilities**, ensuring sustained performance and readiness for executive leadership.

The **Wellbeing Vaccine** is crucial for managers aspiring to executive roles because **leaders who prioritize physical, mental, and emotional health sustain performance, make better decisions, and model balance for their teams.**

Here's a **story** first, followed by **Prescription**.

Story: "Meera and the Wellbeing Vaccine"-T*hriving Without Burning Out*

Meera was a high-performing senior marketing manager at a global FMCG firm. She consistently delivered exceptional results but often worked late nights, skipped meals, and neglected exercise and personal time. Over time, she noticed fatigue, stress, and reduced creativity.

Recognizing the danger, Meera decided to take her **Wellbeing Vaccine**.

Steps she implemented:

1. **Prioritize Health:** She committed to regular exercise, balanced meals, and adequate sleep.
2. **Set Boundaries:** She defined work hours and created personal time for family and hobbies.
3. **Manage Stress:** She adopted mindfulness practices, meditation, and short breaks during workdays.
4. **Delegate and Optimize:** She entrusted tasks to capable team members to avoid overload.
5. **Monitor Balance:** She periodically assessed energy, stress, and satisfaction levels to adjust routines.

The results were remarkable. Meera became more focused, creative, and productive. Her team noticed her positive energy and resilience. Leadership recognized her ability to deliver results consistently without compromising health, making her a trusted candidate for senior roles. Within a year, she was promoted to director, and her wellbeing practices positioned her for executive-level responsibilities with sustainable performance.

Reflecting on her journey, Meera said:

"High performance isn't about working 24/7; it's about maintaining energy, focus, and balance. Wellbeing is the foundation of a lasting career."

Prescription for Corporate Managers to Build the Wellbeing Vaccine

In today's hyperconnected and rapidly evolving world, technology has become the heartbeat of every successful enterprise. Managers who build technological resilience future-proof themselves and their teams against disruption.

The *Technology Vaccine* empowers leaders to stay ahead of the curve, leverage innovation, and drive digital transformation with confidence.

Each dose strengthens your immunity against digital stagnation and builds a foundation for sustained excellence.

Dose 1: Stay Updated on Trends — Awareness Is the First Immunity

To thrive in a digital age, knowledge must evolve as quickly as technology itself.

Monitor emerging trends such as artificial intelligence, automation, analytics, blockchain, and cloud computing. Join industry forums, read reports, and engage with innovation-driven communities.

Being informed enables you to make proactive decisions rather than reactive adjustments.

Take daily — staying current prevents technological obsolescence.

Dose 2: Invest in Learning — Strengthen Your Digital Muscles

Digital fluency begins with self-development.

Enroll in relevant online programs, certifications, and executive tech workshops to understand modern tools and systems. Continuous learning keeps your thinking sharp and your leadership relevant.

A learning manager inspires a learning culture.

Take quarterly — professional growth is your long-term immunity booster.

Dose 3: Implement Digital Solutions — Transform Knowledge into Execution

Learning without application weakens your digital immunity.

Identify processes that can be streamlined through automation or AI. Integrate productivity tools, CRM systems, or data platforms to simplify decision-making and reporting.

Execution transforms theory into measurable business outcomes.

Take per project — digital action creates visible transformation.

Dose 4: Upskill Your Team — Spread the Immunity

Technology adoption succeeds only when everyone can use it effectively.

Conduct regular workshops, create internal digital champions, and encourage hands-on learning. Empower your team to navigate tools confidently and explore new ones independently.

When the team grows, the organization strengthens.

Take monthly — collective digital fluency ensures sustained immunity.

Dose 5: Leverage Data for Decisions — Replace Guesswork with Insight

Data-driven decision-making is the backbone of modern leadership.

Use analytics dashboards and performance metrics to assess trends, predict outcomes, and validate choices. Allow data to guide resource allocation, goal setting, and innovation strategies.

When intuition aligns with evidence, results multiply.

Take before major decisions — data sharpens strategic accuracy.

Dose 6: Showcase Impact — Measure and Communicate Results

Highlight the measurable value of your technological initiatives.

Show leadership how digital adoption reduces cost, improves speed, enhances customer experience, or drives revenue. Quantify outcomes to secure future investment and inspire team commitment.

Visibility accelerates transformation.

Take after implementation — results validate your digital leadership.

Dose 7: Experiment and Innovate — Build a Culture of Curiosity

Innovation is the booster dose of progress.

Encourage pilot projects, sandbox testing, and rapid prototyping of new tools. Create a safe environment where experimentation is celebrated, not feared.

Each experiment, whether successful or not, contributes to organizational intelligence.

Take continuously — innovation prevents stagnation.

Dose 8: Collaborate Across Functions — Build a Connected Ecosystem

Technology thrives when silos fall.

Collaborate with HR, finance, marketing, and operations to integrate digital systems and share insights. Cross-functional synergy reduces redundancy and boosts efficiency.

True digital transformation is an organizational, not departmental, achievement.

Take collaboratively — shared learning multiplies impact.

Dose 9: Prepare for Change — Strengthen Your Adaptive Response

Every digital evolution demands mindset evolution.

Encourage your team to embrace change, stay open to new tools, and overcome fear of the unknown. Lead with transparency during transitions and support your people emotionally and practically.

Adaptability ensures survival through disruption.

Take during every transition — flexibility is your shield against resistance.

Dose 10: Integrate Strategy with Technology — Align Purpose with Progress

Technology is only powerful when it serves strategic goals.

Ensure every new system, tool, or platform aligns with organizational vision, performance metrics, and customer value. Strategic integration turns technology from a cost into a catalyst for success.

Digital transformation must always serve business transformation.

Take at the strategic level — alignment ensures long-term digital vitality.

Recommended Dosage:

Administer one dose at every stage of your digital journey. Reinforce with periodic training and innovation reviews. Combine with doses of empathy, ethics, and adaptability for holistic corporate immunity.

Side effects include improved efficiency, faster decision-making, enhanced innovation, and sustained relevance in a tech-driven world.

Executives are defined not just by results, but by their ability to sustain performance over the long term.

The Wellbeing Vaccine ensures managers remain healthy, energized, and resilient while building a career immune to burnout.

Leaders who cultivate wellbeing inspire their teams, make better decisions, and secure sustainable executive growth.

CAREER IMMUNITY HANDBOOK – 30 VACCINES FOR FULL CAREER IMMUNITY

#	Vaccine	Story Essence	Key Prescription	One-Line Takeaway
1	Experience Vaccine	Learning through tough projects accelerates growth.	Volunteer for challenging assignments, learn from mistakes, seek feedback.	Hands-on experience is the fastest career accelerator.
2	Process Vaccine	Mastering SOPs prevents errors and builds credibility.	Learn policies, follow processes consistently, guide juniors.	Know the rules to play smart and professional.
3	Ego-Neutralizer Vaccine	Handling toxic people without absorbing negativity preserves focus.	Respond professionally, practice empathy, maintain positivity.	Protect your energy; don't take negativity personally.

#	Vaccine	Story Essence	Key Prescription	One-Line Takeaway
4	Networking Vaccine	Early networking opens doors and support systems.	Build genuine relationships, attend events, maintain connections.	Networks accelerate learning, collaboration, and growth.
5	Skill-Upgradation Vaccine	Continuous learning ensures relevance.	Learn emerging skills, apply them, share knowledge.	Staying current is the ultimate career shield.
6	Mentorship Vaccine	Guidance from seniors avoids pitfalls and speeds promotion.	Identify mentors, implement feedback, maintain relationships.	Mentors amplify your growth trajectory.
7	Time-Management Vaccine	Effective time management prevents burnout.	Prioritize tasks, use tools, focus, review schedules.	Manage time; multiply impact.
8	Resilience Vaccine	Recovering from setbacks strengthens long-term success.	Embrace failures, maintain positivity, seek support.	Resilience turns setbacks into stepping stones.

#	Vaccine	Story Essence	Key Prescription	One-Line Takeaway
9	Conflict-Resolution Vaccine	Resolving disputes maintains harmony and trust.	Listen actively, focus on interests, seek win-win outcomes.	Calm resolution builds influence and trust.
10	Financial-Literacy Vaccine	Money management secures freedom and strategic decisions.	Track finances, plan savings, understand taxes, invest wisely.	Financial literacy protects your career and future.
11	Adaptability Vaccine	Embracing change ensures success in new environments.	Stay flexible, learn cultural norms, build cross-functional relationships.	Adaptability makes you indispensable.
12	Feedback Vaccine	Constructive criticism fuels growth.	Listen, clarify, implement, show progress.	Feedback is your personal growth accelerator.
13	Communication Vaccine	Clear communication reduces errors and boosts influence.	Tailor messages, listen actively, confirm understanding.	Effective communication is a leadership cornerstone.
14	Visibility Vaccine	Showcasing achievements prevents invisibility.	Share successes tactfully, volunteer for visible projects.	If you don't showcase value, no one will notice it.

#	Vaccine	Story Essence	Key Prescription	One-Line Takeaway
15	Innovation Vaccine	Creativity in repetitive roles drives impact.	Identify gaps, propose solutions, encourage ideation.	Innovation keeps your career fresh and relevant.
16	Strategic-Thinking Vaccine	Long-term perspective creates value beyond tasks.	Link work to goals, anticipate risks, share insights.	Think strategically to become a valued decision-maker.
17	Personal-Branding Vaccine	A unique identity amplifies credibility and influence.	Highlight strengths, share knowledge, engage professionally.	Your brand precedes your designation.
18	Collaboration Vaccine	Breaking silos strengthens results and relationships.	Encourage teamwork, share credit, build trust.	Collaboration multiplies impact and visibility.
19	Delegation Vaccine	Smart delegation prevents overload and develops teams.	Assign tasks wisely, provide guidance, trust execution.	Delegate to grow yourself and your team.
20	Opportunity-Seeking Vaccine	Spotting hidden opportunities accelerates growth.	Volunteer for projects, evaluate impact, take calculated risks.	Proactivity creates career acceleration.

#	Vaccine	Story Essence	Key Prescription	One-Line Takeaway
21	Decision-Making Vaccine	Timely, confident decisions build credibility.	Define options, assess risks, decide, learn from outcomes.	Effective leaders act decisively.
22	Empathy Vaccine	Understanding others strengthens loyalty and trust.	Listen actively, acknowledge challenges, adapt leadership style.	Empathy transforms teams and leadership effectiveness.
23	Crisis-Management Vaccine	Calm leadership in crises builds trust.	Assess objectively, prioritize, communicate, learn.	Leaders shine brightest under pressure.
24	Influence Vaccine	Persuasion ensures people listen and align.	Build credibility, communicate persuasively, foster trust.	Influence is the currency of leadership.
25	Cultural-Sensitivity Vaccine	Respecting diversity enhances global collaboration.	Learn norms, adapt styles, promote inclusivity.	Cultural intelligence enables global leadership.
26	Vision Vaccine	Inspiring clarity aligns teams toward long-term goals.	Define goals, connect work to strategy, engage teams.	Vision transforms direction into impact.

#	Vaccine	Story Essence	Key Prescription	One-Line Takeaway
27	Ethics Vaccine	Integrity safeguards reputation and long-term success.	Be transparent, follow governance, mentor ethically.	Ethics protect your career and legacy.
28	Negotiation Vaccine	Fair deals protect value and relationships.	Prepare, define priorities, seek win-win, maintain composure.	Negotiation secures organizational and personal credibility.
29	Technology Vaccine	Embracing AI & digital tools prevents obsolescence.	Stay updated, implement tools, upskill, align with strategy.	Technology competence future-proofs your career.
30	Wellbeing Vaccine	Balance health, family, and career for sustainable performance.	Prioritize health, set boundaries, delegate, reflect regularly.	Wellbeing is the foundation of lasting career success.

How to Use This Handbook Summary

1. **Quick Reference:** Use this table to review all 30 vaccines at a glance.
2. **Self-Assessment:** Identify which vaccines you have mastered and which need attention.
3. **Action Plan:** Implement **Prescription** for each vaccine systematically to build full career immunity.
4. **Career Growth:** Combine these skills to survive challenges, thrive under pressure, and accelerate promotion to executive leadership.

Full career immunity is not luck — it's deliberate, consistent cultivation of skills, mindset, and resilience.

By taking these 30 doses, you are equipping yourself to survive, thrive, and leave a lasting impact in the corporate world.